When you can't pray

can't

FINDING HOPE WHEN YOU'RE
NOT EXPERIENCING GOD

AL TRUESDALE

Front cover image: Corbis
Printed in Malta by Interprint
ISBN 1-85345-349-8

CONTENTS

ACKNOWLEDGMENTS

I relied on the assistance of numerous people in the creation of this book. During the writing process, members of a focus group read and critiqued each chapter. I am deeply indebted to these focus group members who gave liberally of their time and careful attention: Rick Barber, a steam turbine engineer in Charlotte, North Carolina; Karen Kaufman, an investment associate in Lake Wylie, South Carolina; Vicki Miller, a wife, mother and eucharistic minister in the Roman Catholic Church, Salisbury, Maryland; Charles R. Millhuff, an evangelist in the Church of the Nazarene, Olathe, Kansas; Susan Middendorf of Overland Park, Kansas, registrar at Nazarene Theological Seminary, Kansas City; Ward Williams, a portfolio manager in a Kansas investment firm and a lay leader in his church; and Elizabeth Truesdale, a financial services agent in Kansas City.

I am also deeply indebted to my wife, Esther, for painstakingly reading and critiquing all the chapters. For more than 30 years she has helped me hammer rough drafts into readable pieces. She is the one who looks at me and says, 'People won't have the slightest idea what you're talking about. You need to work on this some more.' And so I do.

My appreciation also extends to Jeanette Littleton of Beacon Hill Press of Kansas City, who has patiently edited the manuscript.

INTRODUCTION

For many Christians prayer is a vibrant and fulfilling part of their lives. We should celebrate this fact and thank God. This book is not written particularly for those people. Rather, it's written for Christians who try to pray and can't. They may be new Christians or may have known Christ for a long time. The problem is not that they have no interest in prayer, but that they find it very difficult or pointless. Prayer may seem so frustrating that they've almost given up on it.

When we can't engage in satisfying prayer, we may feel excluded from the ranks of acceptable Christian discipleship. We assume that with proper guidance all Christians can practise successful communion with God. People who can't achieve these goals can feel like lepers in the Church.

When You Can't Pray challenges these assumptions. It speaks to children of God who know they are faithful to their Lord but find prayer to be a major obstacle. For some Christians, mention of prayer dredges up memories of failures. It may remind them of personal or family struggles that have made prayer a barrier to overcome rather than a dependable path to walk. For others prayer is at best the means by which an anguished disciple can mutter questions, doubts and fears to the Lord. These people live in the shadow of personal despair.

This book includes in God's family many people for whom a call to prayer is a signal to head for the exits. They are very uncomfortable in the presence of Christians who speak of rich communion with God through prayer. This book is about prayer 'for those who can't'. We will listen to these people. And we will hear from the God of grace. God is indeed the God we Christians confess Him to be and to which the Bible bears witness. His faithfulness is stronger than the failures that ambush us. Because Christian hope is all the New Testament claims, it has far more to do with God holding us than with our holding Him.

In the confidence that God is unmatched in His holiness, love and mercy and that He is not frightened by honest people, we will give voice to those who cannot pray. We will let doubt, disenchantment, tragedy and even anger speak – just as the Bible does. We will also give full voice to grace and Christian hope as authored by our Lord Jesus Christ.

One of the many people for whom this book is written is the individual who wrote the following letter to her pastor. Shelley is a young mother of three. The middle child has cancer. Radiation is exhausting the family financially and emotionally. Shelley's husband is not a Christian. For more than a year Shelley and her children have marginally attended the church my friend pastors. She and her husband struggle to communicate.

Pastor,

Thanks so much for your encouragement. Sometimes that's all I need to get through another day. Reading your letter this morning set off a bunch of emotions. I hope you don't mind, but I'm about to lay them all on you.

I wish so much that I had the faith you talk about ... I'm trying so hard to find my way, but I seem to keep getting lost. I remember that not so long ago you gave a sermon about what a true Christian is. I felt it was my cue to ... leave. But I stayed and listened and wondered if I could ever be like what you described. You certainly weren't describing any part of me ... I don't feel ... I am a bad person, but definitely someone who is very confused with a lot of unsolved issues ...

Thank you for praying for me. It's pretty sad, but

I'm still not sure how to pray for myself. When I do try, I often wonder if anyone is listening. I sure don't feel like it. Jim and I are so in debt right now that every day I wonder, *When will it get better?* I have to scrape to find something to make for dinner for my children three or four times a week. I worry about which one I will have to take to the doctor next – and if the doctor will even see them because we owe so much in doctor's bills. Every time we think things might be a little better next week, something else happens to discourage us ...

–Shelley

01

When prayer loses its meaning

Elaine had been a Christian most of her life. A graduate from theological college and now a business professional, she knew the language of the Christian faith. She had even taken a course in spiritual formation. But on this day Elaine had not come to lunch with me to display her doctrinal knowledge. She wanted to discuss problems in her spiritual life.

'I think I'm losing my faith,' she announced.

That was surprising news. I waited for an explanation. She said, 'I can't pray.' Many of the concepts, words and requests she had heard about prayer presented obstacles to her spiritual growth and communion with God.

On the one hand she had been taught to believe in what she calls 'all the *omnis*' – God's omnipotence (all power), omniscience (all knowledge), and omnipresence (presence everywhere). On the other hand, as a child growing up, she had seen a functional understanding of prayer that indicated that 'God is not to be bothered until big problems occur'. According to this philosophy, she observed, 'God gave us a brain to use, so we use it. God has more pressing things to deal with than your everyday interests. Don't bother Him with trivial stuff. Read the Bible, respond to God's love and mercy in worship, and work diligently to impact those around you. But don't bother God until you need Him for a really big crisis.'

Because Elaine saw prayer modelled as something you do only in crises, she now struggles to discover the *God of relationship.*

CARL'S STORY

A husband of 23 years and a Christian since childhood, Carl had prayed fervently that his wife would be healed of the liver cancer sapping her life. The books he read, the prayer seminars he attended, and his trusted friends assured him that his wife's healing depended on the quality and intensity of his faith. If his faith were sufficiently strong, God would certainly heal Leatha.

After months of his hoping and praying despite the doctors' worsening diagnoses, Leatha died. Drained of energy and spiritual strength, Carl was not prepared for the accusations he faced. Nor was he prepared for the superficial explanations for Leatha's death that fell freely from the lips of friends who had not shouldered grief such as his. One 'comforter' said God had taken Leatha to strengthen Carl's reliance upon Him. Only Carl knew how intensely he had prayed and how strong his faith had been.

No sooner had Carl begun to recover from Leatha's death than he learned his 18-year-old son, Raymond, was suffering from leukaemia. Carl knew, and his friends assured him, that God was too good to allow Raymond's death. Leatha's death had sorely tested him. But now he would see the 'salvation of the Lord' in Raymond's healing. On his son's behalf, Carl claimed all the Bible's promises, even making long lists of verses he thought God had given for signs of healing. He acted upon his faith and refused to think of Raymond as having anything but a healthy future. He continued to set aside money for his son's college years.

Clearly, with so many prayers being offered on his behalf, only time separated Raymond from a restoration to health. In church services, prayer groups and in conversations, Carl heard that God was bound to honour His promises. At times he wondered about the language. It seemed to turn God into a puppet. But he repeatedly heard these words. So Carl put aside his questions and shored up weak spots in his faith.

On a cold, rainy, February afternoon, 18 months after the initial diagnosis, Carl sat beside Raymond's grave as a 'religiously' devastated man who had exhausted his spiritual resources. Like Job, Carl had not failed God. This much he knew. The language of prayer and faith that seemed so easy for others and that promised such a balm for him was now bankrupt.

As the minister spoke of resurrection faith, Carl slowly burned. As he was being expected to show hope, he was seized by a gnawing doubt, even contempt, for prayer and faith. He wanted to escape. God and resurrection seemed to him like grotesque mockeries of simple, believing people such as him.

Carl started loathing his Christian friends' superficial though sincere responses to his tortured soul. His pastor visited him and with good intentions urged him to pray more. From within the darkened corridors of his soul, Carl responded with steely resolve, 'Pastor, I neither can nor want to pray.'

Many Christians have never experienced pain remotely similar to what Elaine and Carl have endured. Some people might say they need to correct their attitudes and get rid of their self-pity. The problem lies with them, they say. Elaine has been victimised by her mind, Carl by his emotions.

I believe Elaine and Carl's questions are far more substantial and should not be dismissed. And the answers to their questions lie much deeper than simply attributing their questioning to a deceptive mind and fragile emotions. Superficial 'try harder' solutions completely miss both the pain and the source of their anguish. Though critics may never understand, prayer had broken down for both of them.

A person might quickly answer that Elaine and Carl both have a faulty understanding of prayer. This is probably true. But for them, the obstructions are real and should be taken seriously. Both are attempting to live as Christians according to roadmaps that are leading them away from God, not towards Him.

For these and additional reasons, many Christians find it difficult, if not impossible, to pray meaningfully and intelligently. If God is as big as the Bible makes Him out to be, then He will be able to entertain their frustrations, their anger and their doubts. And eventually He will lead them through the darkness. In fact, the Bible tells of many people like Elaine and Carl.

HABAKKUK'S STORY

If Elaine and Carl could have visited Jerusalem in the late seventh century BC, they might have met a strange prophet named Habakkuk and found in him someone who understood and shared their questions. Habakkuk's story can be one of the most helpful stories in the Old Testament. To understand him, let's review some events that led up to his controversy with God.

During Habakkuk's time, death stalked Judah. Habakkuk was a zealot for the pure worship of God. He was deeply devoted to the great revival that King Josiah initiated (the Deuteronomic Reformation), told in 2 Kings 22 and 2 Chronicles 34. Josiah had come to the throne with a strong love for God, His Law and the Temple. The revival was an impressive effort to eliminate all pagan worship. Josiah wanted to restore a sincere worship of God.

Amon was the king who preceded Josiah. Before Amon was Manasseh, the villain of Judah. He had given in to the Assyrians by reopening the pagan shrines outside Jerusalem. Earlier, his father, Hezekiah, had destroyed the pagan shrines and practices. But Manasseh tried to combine the worship of Yahweh with the worship of Baal. The people of Judah began to worship Yahweh at the altars of Baal. An emblem of the mother goddess was created, and sacred prostitution was practised (2 Kings 23:7).

Manasseh had also promoted worship of the heavenly bodies and introduced pagan practices into the Temple. As a final surrender to paganism, he and the people practised human sacrifice. Manasseh actually burned his own son as a pagan offering (Jer. 7:31).

In contrast, Josiah removed all signs of Assyrian domination and pagan influence. He also wanted to restore a united kingdom, with Jerusalem as the capital. Josiah's first efforts at reform began in 629 BC, the 12th year of his reign (2 Chron. 34:3). The revival was well underway when in the 18th year (621 BC) a remarkable discovery was made. While making repairs to the Temple and cleansing it of pagan objects, workers found a manuscript – the Book of the Law (Torah).

When the manuscript (probably Deuteronomy 12–26) was

read to Josiah, he tore his garments in despair. He asked the high priest to verify the authenticity of the document. The high priest consulted Huldah the prophetess. Her response cut to the nation's heart: because Judah had grossly violated the covenant, God would bring evil upon Jerusalem.

Shaken over how extensively Judah had sinned, Josiah called the people to the Temple. He read to them 'the Book of the Covenant' the workers had found. The people renewed their covenant with God and promised to obey His commandments. A great nationwide reform followed.

Josiah implemented the revival with even greater thorough-ness than that of Hezekiah. Paganism was abolished. Canaanite Baal worship, worship of the heavenly bodies, and worship of other deities ended. Out of the Temple and onto the junk pile went all alien objects. The people stopped 'sacred prostitution', child sacrifice and consulting of wizards.

Josiah destroyed the outlying sanctuaries, hotbeds of paganism. Their idolatrous priests were put to flight. Josiah even extended the revival into the old Northern Kingdom. He destroyed the temple of Bethel and concentrated worship of Yahweh in the renewed Jerusalem Temple. From there the official priesthood could make sure pagan practices did not taint worship of God.

But the doctrine that supported the revival held a serious flaw. It oversimplified God's ways and made divine justice too neat. The people were told that if only they obeyed the Law, all would go well for them. If they did not, they would face hardship. According to the teaching, the people of Judah would receive success or failure, rewards or punishments, calculated by how obedient they were to a code of rules.[1]

The covenant was twisted into a sure-fire way to 'get some-thing out of' religion. Living through this period, Jeremiah accused the religious authorities of using their pens to turn the Law into a lie (Jer. 8:8).

During Josiah's reforms, the sprawling Assyrian Empire was slipping out of control. After 652 BC, the flames of revolt spread to Egypt and Babylon. The death of the Assyrian Empire came in 612 BC. Nineveh, the Assyrian capital, fell to a combined attack from the Babylonians, Medes and Scythians. The Assyrians made an unsuccessful last-ditch stand at Haran.

Then came a turn of events that only raw political interests can explain. Pharaoh Neco (610–594 BC) decided to try to rescue Assyria, Egypt's former enemy. He thought Egypt would be better off with a weak Assyria than with a strong Babylon. So in 609 BC he marched north to salvage the remnants of the Assyrian Empire.

Meanwhile in Jerusalem, Josiah heard of Neco's move. He decided to side with Babylon, hoping this would help him achieve his goal of uniting the kingdom of David. So he marched his army north to the pass of Megiddo, where he intended to stop the Egyptians and win Babylon's favour.

Things did not go as planned. Josiah was defeated and executed at the battle of Megiddo. The grand plan had collapsed. Now good King Josiah, author of the great revival, friend of God and not yet 40 years old, was dead. The cruel events shattered the 'bargain counter' calculations behind the popular motives for the revival. Disillusionment set in. The Egyptians turned Judah into one of its vassal states, and Pharaoh Neco continued his march to the Euphrates. The Egyptians ended up being crushed by the Babylonians.

In Judah, a Babylonian yoke replaced the Assyrian yoke. The new one was no lighter or more merciful than the old one.

What happened to the great revival? It collapsed. As events demonstrated and as Jeremiah realised, the revival had not resulted in a circumcision of the heart (Deut. 10:16). It did not survive its shallow roots. Within 20 years almost all signs of revival had vanished. The accomplishments were gone. Mosaic faith was forgotten. And worship of God once again blended into worship of pagan deities.

Where does Habakkuk fit into this picture? He had seen it all. He had seen the spiritual rot from Manasseh's apostasy. He had experienced great hope for his country under Josiah's leadership. He had cheered the great reforms that seemed to sweep paganism from the land and had rejoiced to see the Temple restored. But he had also listened as the 'gospel' of predictable returns was preached.

Habakkuk painfully absorbed the trauma of Josiah's defeat and execution and watched the great revival collapse. Who could question that God had inspired Josiah to lead the great revival? Who could doubt that destroying pagan worship would lead the people to even greater faithfulness to God? Habakkuk's hopes had never been greater.

But every hope had been dashed, and his faith was badly shaken. Who could fail to understand Habakkuk's anguish of soul? None of us could gauge his depth of despair. Can we to some extent appreciate his bitter disappointment with God?

What did Habakkuk say to God? How did he now respond to the One he had trusted? Because he was a prophet and authored a book of the Bible, we might expect that he would patiently trust the Lord. He would surely leave for us some exemplary prayers and would become a great model of praise.

Did he? No. The patience, prayers and praise that we might have expected did not surface. *Habakkuk could not pray, could not trust and could no longer hope.* With the collapse of the reformation and with news of the advancing Babylonians, Habakkuk bitterly aired his disappointments:

> O LORD, how long shall I cry for help,
>   and you will not listen?
> Or cry to you 'Violence!'
>   and you will not save?
> Why do you make me see wrongdoing
>   and look at trouble?
> Destruction and violence are before me;
>   strife and contention arise.
> So the law becomes slack
>   and justice never prevails.
> The wicked surround the righteous –
>   therefore judgment comes forth perverted.
> (Hab. 1:2–4, NRSV)

Habakkuk asked God, '[If] your eyes are too pure to behold evil, and [if] you cannot look upon wrongdoing; [then] why do you look on the treacherous, and [why are you] silent when the wicked swallow those more righteous than they?' (1:13, NRSV).

Would any of us dare speak to God that way? Elaine and Carl seem quite mild in comparison.

A CHASTENED FAITH

Paul Ricoeur[2] spoke of a reality common to Elaine, Carl and Habakkuk. He pinpointed a 'first' and a 'second naivety' in Christian faith. We might also call it a first and second level of belief or faith as long as we don't imply two levels of Christians. The first and second naivety have nothing to do with superior or inferior faith. It just describes something that happens to many people for any number of reasons.

Though at first the language might seem strange, you may have experienced what Ricoeur is talking about. For many people – both new and older Christians – the first naivety is characteristic and sufficient. They intensely love God, the Church and others. They faithfully pray, attend church services and support the Christian ministry. They encounter no major problems or questions in their faith. The answers they have received are adequate. Questions about Christianity that bother some people don't trouble them.

The first naivety usually describes a faith that has yet to be tested either by severe trials, complexity, reflection or doubt. The faith of those who live in the first naivety should not be scorned or dismissed. It is authentic faith in Christ. Most of us begin there. Many people remain there, unless something happens to challenge the answers the first naivety provides.

As long as a faith typical of the first naivety is satisfactory, we should be cautious about challenging it. No one should ever disrespect it.

Although I should have known better, I once caused serious unrest for my aged mother-in-law, who was staying with us during the time when Timothy McVeigh was on trial. One evening CNN replayed scenes from the 1995 Oklahoma City bombing. I sat in stunned silence watching scenes of the carnage. My mother-in-law broke the silence by announcing, 'All of that was God's will.'

She spoke with conviction, unaware of the implications about God that her proclamation sparked. Her simple analysis was the only way she could reconcile the sovereignty of God with horrendous evil.

I should have been smart enough to remain silent. I should

have respected her age and 'religious' history. But I didn't. Instead, I 'unloaded'. Visibly shaken, Grandma Blume left the room. That evening, after she told Esther what I had done, I received a lesson in how not to treat an elderly Christian who didn't need more problems sent her way. 'Don't you ever do that again' ended a session I was happy to escape. Grandma Blume was still living in the first naivety.

Teachers who introduce the Bible to college students understand the pain that growing in knowledge can produce. The same can be said for pastors and teachers in the natural sciences, philosophy and theology. For an illustration of how a wise teacher attempted to wrestle with tensions between the first and second naivety, look at how the apostle Paul deftly made peace between those in the Corinthian church who thought it acceptable to eat meat offered to idols and those who thought doing so was idolatrous (1 Cor. 8). We might also listen to Paul explaining the difference between incidentals and substance in the kingdom of God (Rom. 14).

Probably in most instances we don't invite conflicts or crises in the first naivety. Instead, they seem to find us. Tensions steal in ever so subtly. They come uninvited, even though we might at first strongly oppose them. They come because distance, cracks, fissures develop between the answers we have received and the questions that life presents.

For some people, life's questions challenge the adequacy of the first naivety. Such experiences may be prompted by formal education, conversations with friends, a marital failure, a wayward child or a crushing tragedy. Sometimes it happens as one reads the Bible carefully.

Challenges to the first naivety are usually fiercely resisted and may be silenced for a time. After working with students for almost 30 years and from counselling people, I know that life and the mind have a way of pushing questions to the surface again and again. Finally they must be faced. The questions are as varied as are personal spiritual histories. In this chapter we deal with challenges to the first naivety that arise regarding prayer.

Life in the borderland between the first and second naivety can be very lonely, painful and even frightening. Usually we think something's wrong with us and that no one would understand.

When challenges to the first naivety occur, responses can take at least two forms. Many people react in dogged defensiveness. They use their mind to lock all the doors. They search to make sure no more intruders have got in. After a struggle, the reign of the first naivety usually is restored. Peace returns.

After some time, many people enter the second naivety. Painfully, yet bravely, they struggle with disturbing challenges they face. No matter how attractive the old certainty of the first naivety appears, they finally decide they cannot go back. They must go on. Either alone or through mentors, they search for a richer faith, one strong enough to support growth and large enough to house it. They move towards a richer knowledge of God that is broad enough to entertain an advancing faith.

The second naivety does not mean a person leaves his or her faith behind. Instead, it represents a solid embrace of faith. Those who enter the chastened level of faith and the more reflective faith they embrace, are different. Faith is richer, broader, more complex and probably more intense than before. Even with the questions, the centre holds. Faith expands. Some things once stubbornly held have dropped away. And what remains has been refined.

Elaine, Carl and Habakkuk were candidates for the second naivety with reference to prayer. As touching prayer, their first naivety was dissolving and they were not sure what would replace it. Convincing reasons for prayer were evaporating. Each would need another richer level of faith, or the centre would cease to hold. They faced the threat of an eroding orbit of faith and of being captured by some other gravitational pull.

SOME REASONS A CRISIS IN PRAYER HAPPENS

The stories of Elaine, Carl and Habakkuk don't exhaust the reasons why prayer loses its meaning. It happens for some people because they begin to think seriously about the implications of what they and others say when they pray. Let's identify some of the better-known reasons.

First, some people decide prayer is meaningless because they suspect that if God is as our prayers imply, then He must be too lazy and too ignorant to worship. These people are told to ask God to 'help the missionaries' or 'help all the Christian ministers in the world'. Or they may be encouraged to pray that God will give wisdom to public officials or protect children at risk. They are supposed to ask God to heal people who are sick.

Now why, they ask, should we need to encourage God to do what He should be doing anyway? If God sent the missionaries and called the pastors, doesn't He already know they need His assistance? Doesn't He already know when someone is sick or when a child is in danger? Does He not already care for the person? Why prompt Him to do what He already plans to do just because of His faithfulness?

These same people ask, If we know what God should do, and if we need to encourage Him to do it, are we not His moral and mental superiors? Prayer loses its meaning for these people, because it seems senseless.

Second, prayer becomes meaningless for some people because they lose their bearings in the instructions they receive. On the one hand they are to pray for and expect a person to be healed. On the other hand they should pray, 'Thy will be done.' Now which one is it? The two instructions don't seem to reconcile. If God already has a will in the matter, why make a request that might be contrary to it?

And why do we pray for a person's healing when he or she truly wants to depart and be with the Lord?

Third, related to the second question, some people find prayer meaningless because they don't understand how people can speak so easily about 'knowing God's will'. Before an event unfolds they say they know God's will for its outcome. But when things turn out differently than expected, the same people speak of the outcome as having been God's will, ignoring their earlier certainty.

Fourth, some Christians lose their way in prayer because they have a difficult time knowing what to identify as good and what to call evil. So they find it hard to know what they should pray for. It's difficult to know how to offer thanksgiving.

A few years ago Texas Christians prayed that God would deliver them from an impending hurricane. At the same time, Oklahoma cotton farmers prayed for enough rain to save their endangered crops. As things turned out, the people in Texas wondered why God had not delivered them from the hurricane. But the Oklahoma farmers were thanking God for the rains that saved their cotton. The hurricane was the mother of both trial and blessing.

Now how should a person in, say, Kansas, have prayed beforehand? And for what should he or she have given thanks afterwards?

Philip Yancey tells of a Sunday evening church service during which the pastor reported that a plane carrying nine missionaries had crashed in the Alaskan outback earlier the previous week. All had died. Then the pastor introduced a member of the church who had survived an unrelated plane crash that same week. Upon hearing of the narrow escape, the congregation heartily praised God, for they were certain God had providentially intervened. The congregation evidently had no reluctance in giving God credit for saving one man, but aimed no blame at God for 'failing' to save nine other Christians. How did these people know so much about how God does and does not act?[3]

Fifth, the reality and the indiscriminant display of evil in the world paralyses many people's ability to pray. The New Testament speaks of 'the mystery of iniquity' (2 Thess. 2:7, KJV). The random and senseless visitation of moral and natural evil upon some and the random escape from evil by others, leaves some Christians disorientated. They don't know how to ask God to intercede. Given the unpredictable patterns of evil, what sense does it make to ask for God's intervention either for others or for ourselves? How can we speak intelligently about either a negative or positive outcome of events? What real difference does prayer make anyway?

Sixth, Marjorie Suchocki discusses an obstacle to prayer that some of us might overlook. Given the immensity of the universe and our own insignificance in it, how sensible is it to say that God is concerned about 'me, my needs, my prayers'? Perhaps in earlier times when people believed the earth was the centre of the universe, the question would not have surfaced. When the earth was the focal point, prayer seemed to be more natural.

Now, however, we know that the earth is only one planet in a small solar system and that our solar system is just part of a galaxy we call the Milky Way – a whirling pinwheel made of 100 billion or more stars. There are at least tens of billions of galaxies. So what sense does it make to say that the God who created and runs all of this is concerned about one human who occupies just one speck of space and time?[4]

Seventh, for some people, prayer loses its meaning because the God to whom they pray seems to be just one more tribal deity (bigger of course). God's interests and power seem to be limited to very narrow regions. By some of the prayers we offer in church, for example, it would seem that God's interests are no larger than our own family, denomination, nation, class, race, gender or physical needs. After all, it seems God uses His power to protect the interests of a small part of earth's population. When Christians survive a train wreck, for example, God was protecting them. But what about the Muslims and Buddhists on board who died? Were they simply outside of God's interests, 'collateral damage'? Did they not deserve protection too?

For some Christians, a tribal deity, no matter how big, is still a limited god. A finite god would be unworthy of our worship. He could not be the Creator and Lord of the universe. On the other hand, if God is equally concerned about all people, if He really does make the sun to shine on the just and the unjust, then what is the special benefit of being a Christian?

Confronting the 'God' who is finally nothing more than a tribal deity with limited interests is perhaps the most tenacious struggle with idolatry we will have. Jesus' disciples struggled with this. Many Christians today never get beyond a tribal deity. But before the true God can reign in us, the old tribal deity must die. Short of that, 'God' remains a domestic hearth deity expected to perform household chores on command.

Mark Twain's famous 'War Prayer' was submitted to *Harper's Bazaar*, rejected, and then published after his death in 1923. In this classic writing, Twain exposed the absurdity of praying to a tribal deity. Twain tells of one Sunday morning in a Northern congregation during the United States Civil War. 'It was a time of great and exalting excitement. The country was up in arms, the war was on, in every breast burned the holy fire of patriotism.'

In one church, the building was full of people, including volunteers, 'their young faces alight with martial dreams'.

Eventually the time arrived for the great pastoral prayer. The thrust of the prayer was that an ever-merciful and benign Father would watch over the noble young soldiers. The supplication was that God would aid, comfort and encourage the volunteers in their patriotic work. God should bless them, shield them in the day of battle and hour of peril. He should hold them in His mighty hand, make them strong, confident and invincible. In the bloody onset, God should help them crush the foe. He should grant to them and to their flag and country everlasting honour and glory.

An aged stranger entered and moved slowly up the aisle, his eyes fixed on the minister. His robe reached his feet. His head was bare and his white hair descended to his shoulders. Not conscious of the stranger's presence, the pastor continued to pray, ending with a fervent appeal: 'Bless our arms, and give us victory, O Lord our God.'

The stranger touched the minister's arm and motioned

him aside. He said, 'I come from the Throne – bearing a message from Almighty God! He has heard the prayer of His servant your shepherd and will grant it if such shall be your desire after I, His messenger, shall have explained to you its [full] import ... For it is like unto many of the prayers of men, in that it asks for more than he who utters it is aware of.'

Here now, the stranger said, is the full import of the pastor's prayer:

O Lord our Father, our young patriots, idols of our hearts, go forth to battle – be Thou near them! With them – in spirit – we also go forth from the sweet peace of our beloved firesides to smite the foe. O Lord our God, help us to tear their soldiers to bloody shreds with our shells; help us to cover their smiling fields with the pale forms of their patriot dead; help us to drown the thunder of the guns with the shrieks of their wounded, writhing in pain; help us to lay waste their humble homes with a hurricane of fire; help us to wring the hearts of their unoffending widows with unavailing grief; help us to turn them out roofless with their little children to wander unfriended the wastes of their desolated land in rags and hunger and thirst, sports of the sun flames of summer and the icy winds of winter, broken in spirit, worn with travail, imploring Thee for the refuge of the grave and denied it – for our sakes who adore Thee, Lord, blast their hopes, blight their lives, protract their bitter pilgrimage, make heavy their steps, water their way with their tears, stain the white snow with the blood of their wounded feet! We ask it, in the spirit of love, of Him Who is the Source of Love, and Who is the ever-faithful refuge and friend of all that are sore beset and seek His aid with humble and contrite hearts. Amen.

After a pause, the stranger told the congregation, 'Ye have prayed it; if ye still desire it, speak! The messenger of the Most High waits.'

Twain concludes the 'War Prayer' with these words: 'It was believed afterward that the man was a lunatic, because there was no sense in what he said.'[5]

02

Intercessory prayer

GOING TO WORK WITH GOD

Perhaps no dimension of prayer presents a greater challenge to many Christians than intercessory prayer. Intercessory prayer involves pleading or making a request to God on behalf of another. In intercessory prayer we ask God to do something that perhaps only He can do.

The Bible contains many instances of intercessory prayer. Jesus Himself is the Great Intercessor. Both the Old and New Testaments clearly show that God expects His people to pray prayers of intercession. The Bible records instances in which prayers of intercession accomplished their intended purposes and instances in which they didn't.

On the surface, the definition, the divine invitation, and the procedure for intercessory prayer, seem to be straightforward. God's people petition Him for something good that only He can accomplish. Then, being the responsive God of sovereign love and power, assuming that the request pleases Him, He acts and the request is granted.

If it were that simple we could just celebrate our victories in intercessory prayer and move on. But intercessory prayer isn't as straightforward as the definition implies. For many Christians, human experience and reflection generate obstacles that turn intercessory prayer into a puzzle. For some, it becomes a source of frustration and conflict, even anger.

Some of these people have responded to the invitation and acted on their privileges as God's children. They have followed the path as they understand it, but their prayers appear to have gone nowhere, simply to have been swallowed up in a heavenly void. The explanation, 'Well, God always answers your prayer in some way even if you don't recognise it', doesn't satisfy.

This is particularly true when they hear great stories about how God complied with an intercessor's petition. 'Why them and not me?' is an understandable question. Does God play favourites? Is He 'on' some days and 'off' others? Or maybe intercessory prayer is God's form of the lottery.

On the other hand, no fewer than six times in one setting God responded favourably to intercessory prayer Father Abraham offered (Gen. 18). One day, by the oaks of Mamre, an ancient sacred place north of Hebron, God told the elderly Abraham that he and Sarah would give birth to a child. After delivering the news, God talked with Abraham about the infamous wickedness of the cities Sodom and Gomorrah.

God told Abraham He intended to destroy both cities. But in a classic story of intercession, Abraham asked God to revise conditions under which He would set aside plans to destroy Sodom, the city in which his nephew, Lot, lived. And God agreed to do so. This happened six times!

At no point did Abraham deny Sodom's wickedness. He just didn't think God should sweep away the righteous with the unrighteous. He diplomatically reminded God of the reputation to which He should be accountable. 'Will not the Judge of all the earth do right?' (v.25).

For other Christians, intercessory prayer presents a serious conflict in what they think they are supposed to believe about God. If God is all-knowing and all-loving; if He is the living God who always faithfully acts, then why should He wait for an appeal from fallible humans? Isn't the thought of intercessory prayer a leftover from an inferior understanding of God that mature Christians should leave behind? What are we to make of a God who needs to be *convinced* to do what He already knows to be good? Who is this God who needs to be informed by finite beings regarding what His daily assignments are? Is not the God that intercessory prayer implies, some Christians wonder, unworthy of either the name 'God' or of worship by intelligent humans?

People in the latter group find intercessory prayer unworthy of serious attention. They leave it to those who need a higher power who has to be cajoled. They leave it to an outdated deity who enjoys watching people grovel before he doles out what they need. It is best left to those who enjoy dabbling in sentiment and whose minds don't require logic.

If intercessory prayer should play a major role in Christian life, then we must confront the conflicts of people in both groups.

QUESTIONS

So what are we to make of intercessory prayer? The Bible repeatedly either urges us to pray intercessory prayers or displays models of intercessory prayer. Think, for example, of Paul's statement in Romans: '... my heart's desire and prayer to God for the Israelites is that they may be saved'

(Rom. 10:1). Paul would not have wasted his time praying for a cause already lost to God.

The Old and New Testaments teach that the holy and all-loving God, who is sovereign and eternal, responds to intercessory prayer. Both Testaments tell us that God invites this kind of prayer.

Let's look at some of the questions Christians raise about intercessory prayer.

First, if the sovereign and unchanging God does what He wants to do, what sense would it make to say that God responds favourably to intercessory prayer? If God is God with an unlimited perspective, and if we are finite humans with only limited perspectives, what meaning could we possibly derive from telling God what we think He should do? When we see the absurdity of a human being telling God what to do, can intercessory prayer still be meaningful?

Doesn't the Bible discourage this kind of 'nonsense'? Listen to the apostle Paul as he instructs the Roman Christians about God's will for Israel: 'But who are you, O man, to talk back to God? "Shall what is formed say to the him who formed it, 'Why did you make me like this?'" Does not the potter have the right to make out of the same lump of clay ...?' (Rom. 9:20–21; see also Isa. 29:16; 45:9; 64:8; Jer. 18:6).

And if we answer, 'Well, we're just urging God to do what He already knows to be best', that creates problems too. Should we call the prime minister daily and urge him to go to work each morning? Should we call the local police to remind them of the importance of patrolling our neighbourhoods? If the response is 'Well, no, but we don't really encourage or instruct God. He would do His will anyway,' then another question surfaces: 'Then why waste the time?'

Second, does intercessory prayer result in changing God's

mind? In Abraham's case, that seemed to be true. And it surely seemed to be true after God, through Isaiah, told King Hezekiah he would die. Hezekiah prayed that God would remember how righteously he had lived. Before Isaiah could reach home, God turned him around and sent him back to tell the king that God had answered his prayer. The new message was that God had decided to tack on another 15 years (2 Kings 20:1–11).

In another instance, after the Israelites had sinned with the golden calf, God told Moses He was very angry with the stubborn Hebrews. He was so angry that He decided to wash His hands of them (Exod. 32:10).

But Moses interceded for the wayward people. He even chided the Lord for being overly angry! '... why should your anger burn against your people ...?' (v.11). Then Moses explained to the Lord that if He were to obliterate the people, then God's own reputation with Pharaoh and the Egyptians would suffer. So Moses counselled God to turn away from His dreaded plan.

God seemed to consider Moses' words. Then 'the LORD relented and did not bring on his people the disaster he had threatened' (v.14).

Consider carefully what it would mean for God to change His mind at the instruction of a finite being. How many conflicting requests should He entertain each day? How would God fairly decide when to change His mind and when not to? Would not the heavenly system blow a lot of fuses? What possible lack of knowledge and righteous intentions could God possess that would need to be supplemented by human instruction and correction?

Upon receiving Moses' counsel, did God change His mind, as the text indicates on the surface? Did God sincerely regret something He intended to do? Or does the text mean that God took a different course of action that was already a possibility? Did Moses simply plead for what God had already intended to do?

At any rate, the question remains: Do intercessory prayers make a difference to God?

Third, maybe all of our questions are in the wrong direction. Maybe God wants us to pray intercessory prayers because it helps us, not Him. Maybe they're something like religious calisthenics, or shadow boxing or a religious treadmill. Maybe the purpose of intercessory prayer is just to improve religious muscle tone.

Or maybe intercessory prayer is just psychologically healthy. Perhaps it helps us to vent our feelings, frustrations and desires before God. He knows all along that He alone is infinite and that our knowledge and perspectives are limited. He already knows best. He nevertheless invites intercessory prayer.

But would a loving God invite us to waste our time on something He knows to be pointless? Would He deceive us? Why would the Scriptures repeatedly tell us that God hears and responds to intercessory prayer if He does not?

Fourth, far more popular is the notion that God wants us to struggle with Him through intercessory prayer so we can strengthen our faith. He already knows what should be done and what He will do. But He engages us in the taxing exercise of intercessory prayer so that when He does finally act, we'll be stronger. And furthermore, what God finally does will mean much more to us.

To illustrate the absurdity of this explanation, permit me to alter a childhood story.

Once when I was a child I suffered so intensely from the

flu that I thought I would die. I asked my mother to call Dr Winters, who made house calls. But my mother refused to call the doctor. Now, all along my loving and 'all-wise' mother knew calling Dr Winters would be best for me. But her reason for delaying was to increase my trust in her. She also hoped that when Dr Winters finally arrived, I would better appreciate the penicillin he would inject.

Does this story make any sense? If not, then neither does the explanation for intercessory prayer I have just offered.

In one parable, Jesus tried to tell us that God isn't like this. Jesus likened God to an unjust judge who finally yielded to the persistent pleas of a widow. The judge vindicated the woman against her adversary. Is that the way our heavenly Father is? Jesus asked. No! He said that God will 'bring about justice for his chosen ones, who cry out to him day and night? Will he keep putting them off? I tell you, he will see that they get justice, and quickly' (Luke 18:7–8).

Fifth, is intercessory prayer a way to test God? Maybe its purpose is to lay down a series of conditions by which God can prove He is God. *Here are the hoops I've come up with, Lord. If You can jump through all of them, I'll believe You're God. Then I'll trust You.*

Does that sound familiar? It should. That's what Satan urged Jesus to do when he tempted Jesus in the wilderness. Satan, who had already demonstrated on a grand scale that he had no faith in God, wanted Jesus to become his team member. So he said to Him, 'Here are some conditions You should present to Your Father. Give Him a chance to prove to You on these terms that He really is God. Let Him prove that You're not about to make a fool of Yourself as You begin Your ministry.'

So Satan wanted Jesus to jump from the pinnacle of the

Temple. This would give the Father a chance to prove that Jesus was indeed the Son of God. To intervene, God could quickly send a band of angels to keep Him from splashing on the paving stones.

What Jesus told Satan should stand as a corrective for Christians for all times. Jesus knew that those who truly worship and trust God don't put Him to the test. 'Jesus answered, "It says: 'Do not put the Lord your God to the test'"' (Luke 4:12).

Intercessory prayer has nothing to do with testing God. Faithlessness does.

Sixth, some have dismissed all these questions and their solutions and have offered a 'better way'. They say God divides the future into events with outcomes that make a real difference to Him and those that don't. We never really know which events God must control or the ones about which He is indifferent. But we can affect the latter events through prayer. Dividing things up this way protects God's sovereignty and the reality of intercessory prayer.

By encouraging us to pray, God wants us to affect things in the second class of events. Obviously only God knows which event belongs to which classification. We don't. But in all situations we're to pray fervently and expectantly. Hopefully we'll connect with the second classification.

Clearly a deity this deceitful would not be worth our worship.

Some Christians seem to be able to answer questions about intercessory prayer in some of the ways we have stated without causing a ripple of discomfort. Others find the explanations repulsive, unworthy of either God or humanity. 'If that's what intercessory prayer means,' they say, 'I won't participate in it. Let those willing to live with either absurdity or a mixed-up "God" go right on praying. I surrender my ticket.'

IS THERE ANYTHING BETTER?

By now we might seem to have exhausted all the options. Maybe it's time to lay aside intercessory prayer. But that would be premature.

The New Testament calls us to practise intercessory prayer.[1] It teaches us that God hears and answers prayer. One of my favourite New Testament texts regarding intercessory prayer is this: 'Is any one of you in trouble? He should pray. Is anyone happy? Let him sing songs of praise. Is any one of you sick? He should call the elders of the church to pray over him and anoint him with oil in the name of the Lord. And the prayer offered in faith will make the sick person well; the Lord will raise him up' (James 5:13–15).

Martin Luther said, 'The Lord is great and high, and therefore He wants great things to be sought from Him and is willing to bestow them so that His almighty power might be shown forth.'[2]

We need to dig more deeply into the Christian meaning of intercessory prayer. Fortunately, some Christian teachers can lead us into a richer and defendable understanding. In some places we may need to put our mental engines in a lower gear, for at some points the gradient may be steep. But hold steady. The results will be worth the effort.

First, let's eliminate one misunderstanding. Theologian John H. Wright says that in speaking of intercessory prayer we must reject any explanation that sounds like magic. Magic is a way to manipulate powers that are larger than humans. It is a way to place those powers under human control.[3]

Much of what is said about intercessory prayer in popular Christianity sounds more like magic than worship. In magic the powers people seek to manipulate can be placed under *controls* that transcend even the powers themselves. If the magician can gain access to the levers of control, he or she can use them over the powers and can gain what he or she wants. No matter how quasi-Christian and quasi-biblical is the language in which magic disguises itself, magic is still magic, not Christian prayer and worship.

To the immature Christian, magic can sound so much like prayer that it actually passes as prayer. Unsuspecting Christian readers snap up whole books on prayer that are little more than magic. Magic is a difficult habit to break.

The Bible gives us no hint that we can manipulate God to serve our interests through intercessory prayer. Intercessory prayer does not produce automatic results or place God under the control of some law external to Him. The proper relationship between God and the one who prays must always be one of worship, and that involves no effort to control God.

The beginning of the Lord's Prayer clarifies this. Intercessory prayer begins and ends in worship and by placing ourselves before God as a sacrifice of praise and service (Rom. 12:1–3). Donald Bloesch says, 'In all Christian prayer the overriding motivation is to glorify God and to discover his will for our lives.'[4]

The acceptable postures of all Christian prayer are love, praise, trust and thanksgiving. Christians who pray this way will recognise the foolishness and faithlessness of treating prayer as a way to constrain God. Unlike magic, no automatic results will come from using appropriate words and gestures.

Second, as one who often encourages Christians to pray, the apostle Paul surprises us when he says we don't even know how to pray. Apparently no Christian should approach God as if he or she already has everything figured out. Instead, Paul says, we should recognise our limitations, our 'weakness', as he puts it. To pray correctly, Christians must pray 'in the Spirit'. They must pray with recognition that in Jesus' name the Holy Spirit takes our sincere but limited petitions and presents them to the Father. The Spirit 'helps us in our weakness. We do not know what we ought to pray for ...' (Rom. 8:26).

Third, as John H. Wright reminds us, the first condition of intercessory prayer is faith.[5] In the New Testament, faith means radical trust in, and submission to, the God who by grace alone justifies and reconciles sinners. Faith involves completely turning away from reliance on our own righteousness, wisdom, craftiness and strength. It means holding steadfastly to God alone.

This is the spirit surrounding Christian prayer. It begins and ends in worship. It leaves behind old 'realities' that are passing away and clings to our faithful God.

The New Testament teaching on prayer assumes the person who approaches God in intercessory prayer is in right relationship with the triune God and with his or her neighbour. Prayer is offered in the name of Jesus and 'in the Holy Spirit' (Jude 20). The Holy Spirit makes the riches of Christ available to us. He unites us to Jesus (Rom. 8:9–11). The Holy Spirit is the risen Lord's gift to all who believe in Him (John 7:37–39; Acts 2:38). He alone makes it possible to call out, 'Abba! Father!' when we address God (Gal. 4:6; Rom. 8:15). The Spirit also joins Christians to their sisters and brothers in Christ and to the Body of our Lord (1 Cor. 12:13; 2 Cor. 13:14; Eph. 4:3–4).

Fourth, Wright reminds us of an important point we often forget: if we pray guided by the New Testament, then we don't pray alone. Through the covenant of Christ's shed blood, each of us is a child of God. He calls us by name. But we're also members of the new covenant as members of His Body, the Church. We're members of each other.

All this means that none of us stands as a *lone* individual before God. We're before Him as sisters and brothers of each other and of Jesus Christ. Our sisters and brothers are God's gifts to us, and we to them. We're privileged and commanded to bear one another's burdens and in this way to fulfil the law of Christ (Gal. 6:2). To pray as Christians is to pray for the good of Christ's Body, for its life and ministry everywhere.[6]

We can still have the freedom and urgency to offer petitions for family members or ourselves. But we need to be careful that these do not become the centre of prayer. Intercession should be kindled far more by a longing for God to complete His kingdom among us than for our own particular needs, trials and desires.

To repeat, our own needs should certainly be presented to the Lord. When a child is critically ill we would expect a Christian parent to appeal to the Lord for help. But our needs and the needs of those near us should not become our primary interest as Christians. When this happens, prayer becomes introverted and myopic. It becomes a series of private, disjointed lists shipped to heaven, unrelated to any larger work the Lord is doing.

If the gospel of Christ is to accomplish anything in us, it is to redirect our lives in the direction of something larger. The coming of the kingdom of God in Jesus Christ does not eliminate individuals. But it does set us free from slavery to self-centred living. Becoming a part of God's kingdom sets us free to pray and work for God's peace on earth, for mercy and justice to become the order of human life everywhere.

Fifth, as Donald Bloesch explains,[7] God takes His people seriously in intercessory prayer. They are His covenant partners. This will make no sense to those who think God sits outside history, alone in His sovereignty, completeness and knowledge. A God who doesn't take His people or events seriously simply is not the God of the Bible.

'Covenant' means that God has not chosen to be aloof. Although we can never explain it, the free, triune God has entered a bond with us. His sovereignty is not displayed by dismissing us, but by making us His covenant partners. The triune God, who is already a community of love, invites us into community with Him through our Lord Jesus Christ. Is this beyond our comprehension? Yes, as much as God's wisdom and knowledge are 'unsearchable' (Rom. 11:33).

Unlike the dead idols Isaiah and Jeremiah ridiculed, the God of the Bible listens. He answers. He is the living God. Karl Barth, a major Christian theologian of the twentieth century, said, 'Prayer exerts an influence upon God's action, even upon his existence. This is what the word "answer" means.'[8]

Let's go even deeper into something that makes little sense for many. In this covenant relationship, both the divine and human partners add something essential – both God and we His children are enriched. Deny this, and 'relationship' becomes a meaningless, one-sided term. To say that prayer influences God has *everything to* do with mutual, covenant love, and *nothing* to do with coaxing, cajoling, controlling or manipulating God.

Now we need to emphasise that in this covenant relationship, God remains God. He is the One who makes the covenant possible. It is not made between equals. But God is absolutely trustworthy. We know He will always be faithful to us, because He is always faithful to Himself. He will never fail to be who He is – the triune God of holy love.

As Christians, we know this because the heavenly Father was faithful to Himself by being faithful to His Son. He suffered with His Son. And He raised our Lord from the grave on the third day. Jesus is the New Covenant. Therefore we also know God will be faithful to complete the kingdom Jesus inaugurated.

On this basis, Bloesch tells us, 'Prayer is not simply petition, but strenuous petition. It is not just passive surrender, but active pleading with God ... It consists not merely in reflection on the promises of God, but in taking hold of these promises.'[9]

Intercessory prayer does not set out to change God's purposes. Instead, beyond all human explanation, out of a divinely initiated partnership, intercessory prayer helps to empower and accomplish God's purposes. Call this 'filial reciprocity'.[10]

Intercessory prayer unleashes God's purposes on earth, even as they are in heaven.[11] William Law said prayer is a mighty instrument, 'not for getting man's will done in heaven', but 'for getting God's will done on earth'.[12] Striving with God in intercessory prayer helps us discover the broader scope of His will.

The fulfilment of God's will on earth is at least partly contingent on our prayers. Bloesch says, 'There are several ways in which God's will can be implemented, and through prayer we seek to discover the best way.'

If this is so, intercessory prayer becomes the Christian's great calling, responsibility and privilege. It is a great thanksgiving to the God who has made covenant with us in Christ.

Christians don't overpower God. Rather, as we prevail in intercessory prayer, so does He. We're covenant partners who work with Him for the coming of the kingdom on earth. What a high calling is ours as sisters and brothers of Christ![13]

If all of this seems to pass beyond human understanding, then remember that so do the actions of the gracious God. In grace, through intercessory prayer, God *takes us on as His working, contributing junior partners.* Through the prayers of the saints, God acts to accomplish His purposes in the Church and in the world.

In freedom, God binds Himself to His people's prayers.[14] Intercessory prayer opens to us God's resources for witness, for struggling against 'the spiritual forces of evil' (Eph. 6:12), for spiritual discernment (1 Cor. 2:14), and for ministry. John Calvin believed that God advances His kingdom through the prayers of His people and overthrows the powers of darkness.[15]

Understood in this way, intercessory prayer is work, hard work, faithful work, kingdom and vineyard work. The work of intercessory prayer also includes participating in Christ's sufferings. It includes suffering with the God who suffers over His broken world (2 Cor. 1:5; Phil. 3:10; 1 Pet. 4:13).

Indulgent and self-centred people will not be found in these precincts. Elsie Gibson observed that many of us are so impatient that our greatest likelihood of failure lies in giving up because God does not jump to do what we hope.[16]

What can intercessory prayer do? It can open heaven. It can open prison doors (Acts 4:1–31). It can renew the intercessor's spiritual life. Intercessory prayer can cast out fear. It strengthens Christian ministers and missionaries. It can serve the aims of redeeming grace in the world. Intercessory prayer can unleash revival in the Church and launch missionary movements. It can overcome oppressive regimes and establish justice in the land. It can break down the walls of racial, ethnic, gender and age discrimination. Intercessory prayer can do this in societies and in individuals.

What can the work of intercessory prayer – God working with His people – accomplish? Whatever the kingdom of God intends for God's creation. Intercession can give growth in the Church even under persecution. The question is not what God is willing to do or whether He takes us seriously. The question is, 'To what level of intercession is the Church of Christ willing to commit?'

Marjorie Suchocki wraps it up this way. Intercessory prayer teaches us that 'God works with the world as it is in order to bring it to where it can be. Prayer changes the way the world is, and therefore changes what the world can be. Prayer opens the world to its own transformation.'[17]

If intercessory prayer is so rich, why are some parents' prayers answered while others' seem not to be? Why does intercessory prayer by one spouse result in a healed marriage, while the prayer of another does not? Why does a stunning revival of faith break out in China but not in Great Britain?

The questions could be expanded without end. They immediately raise the problem of tenacious evil in the world. To complete our discussion of intercessory prayer, we must confront the persistence of evil, which we will do in Chapter 7.

03

When 'gods' fail

LIKE SCARECROWS IN A CUCUMBER FIELD

God remains; 'gods' collapse. They fail. That's nearly the central message of Isaiah and Jeremiah. Using razor-sharp language, the two prophets cut to ribbons all forms of idolatry practised in Judah or the surrounding nations. In unsurpassable language they praise the Creator God. They speak of Him as the living God who imparts life to all but who does not draw His life from the world. The two prophets ridicule the lifeless 'gods' that must be nailed down to keep them upright!

With brief exceptions, idol worship in the closing days of Judah's existence ate like acid at the covenant upon which Judah was founded. Readers of Isaiah and Jeremiah are usually dismayed over the tenacity of idol worship in the land. The practice seems to have embedded itself deeply into Judah's soul. How pervasive was idolatry? Let Jeremiah answer. 'Your gods have become as many as your towns, O Judah; and as many as the streets of Jerusalem are the altars you have set up to shame, altars to make offerings to Baal' (11:13, NRSV).

Relentlessly, Isaiah and Jeremiah tried to convince kings and common people that idolatry was a fruitless practice, leading only to deception and religious death. In language so withering that no one should have missed it, Jeremiah said, 'Like a scarecrow in a melon patch ... they have no breath in them' (10:5, 14).

As a child, I learned by observing crows that once they figure out it's a scarecrow they're up against, they come in droves. Even crows can eventually work out that a scarecrow is lifeless. It has power only over animals too 'blind' to recognise the truth. But the 'blind' people of Judah couldn't see that idols had only the significance that they, the worshippers, assigned to them.

Isaiah and Jeremiah lampooned the artisans who made idols and those worshipping them. In one account Isaiah used humour to show the absurdity of idolatry. He tells of an idol-maker who selects a tree in the forest. He waits for the tree to mature and then cuts it down. The idol maker burns one half to warm himself and cook his lunch. Then he takes the second half of the tree back to his workshop, where he slowly shapes the dead wood into a human form. Then he places the idol in a shrine, bows down and prays to the idol, 'Save me, for you are my god!' (44:17, NRSV).

Isaiah points out that the foolish idol worshipper is so blind that he cannot see he burned the other half of what he now worships. He doesn't recognise that he could have just as easily burned the half he worships. Isaiah's devastating conclusion is that when the man worships the idol he 'feeds on ashes' (44:20).

Jeremiah and Isaiah never tired of pointing out that idols

don't carry their worshippers; the worshippers have to carry the idols (Isa. 45:20; 46:1–2). In time, both the idols and their makers will descend into confusion (Isa. 45:16).

All of Judah's idols failed. They broke under the weight of national crises. After the destruction of Jerusalem, as the people were preparing to go into exile in Babylon, both nobles and commoners loaded their idols onto 'weary animals' (Isa. 46:1). Finally, Isaiah said, the broken-down gods could carry no one. That, Isaiah and Jeremiah said, is what always happens to gods.

THE GOD WHO DOES NOT FAIL

In contrast to idols, the God who created the heavens and the earth will carry His people – in good times and in bad. Unlike idols, God isn't part of the finite world that breaks down when worshipped. He is the One beside whom there is no other. He is the living God. He is the Saviour. Unlike idols, God doesn't have to be rescued in times of distress.

Unlike the idols that rely on nature and human imagination for their existence, God is the source of His own life. Many people in Jerusalem thought no enemy nation would ever destroy the Temple because then God Himself would cease to be. They foolishly thought God was like a pagan deity who depends upon a temple or nation to exist. Jeremiah applied the brakes to that notion. He told the people that even if Judah and Jerusalem were destroyed, God would live on. Even without a Temple, and even if His people were captive, God would continue to direct the course of history.

TURNING THE SEARCHLIGHT TOWARDS HOME

From our safe distance, it's easy to applaud Isaiah and Jeremiah's judgment against Judah. We wonder, *How could they have been so blind as to worship lifeless products of human hands?* With the prophets, our righteous anger rises to defend the eternal God.

But hold on! The temptation and practice of leaning on gods that finally collapse did not end with the last verses of the Old Testament. The temptation is as real, subtle and insidious today as when Isaiah and Jeremiah walked the streets of Jerusalem. Jeremiah's warning to Judah is equally applicable to us: 'Do not learn the [idolatrous] ways of the nations' (10:2).

Isaiah and Jeremiah said the 'gods' will always fail. They cannot 'listen', and they cannot 'answer'. They can give back to the worshipper only what the worshipper assigns to or invests in them. Finally the investments fail. Eventually the idol worshipper will have to load his or her dumb idols onto a beast of burden and follow them down into the land of 'confusion'.

Let's face it: prayer fails for many of us because we bow before 'gods' of our own making instead of the free, true and living God who inhabits eternity. Will we permit the Holy Spirit to expose the 'gods' to whom we pray and who can give back only what we have given to them? Will we let the living God collapse our 'gods'?

In *The Screwtape Letters*, the old demon, called Screwtape, instructs Wormwood, his nephew, in how to defeat his 'patient' (a new Christian). Wormwood is told not to worry about the fact that his patient is praying. He should just make sure the patient prays to something he has made, 'not to the

Person who has made him'. Wormwood may even encourage him to improve the object he has made. But if the patient ever realises his error and consciously 'directs his prayers "not to what I think thou art but to what thou knowest thyself to be", our situation is, for the most part, desperate.'[1]

IDOLATRY WITHOUT 'IDOLS'

We have often used the word 'idolatry'. What does it really mean?

Idolatry occurs when we elevate a finite thing into the place that belongs to God alone. It means ascribing to something God created the glory that only He should have.

This happens whenever we give ultimate or divine significance to something with limited and perishable importance. Yielding to the temptation to practise idolatry is extremely subtle. It can happen even when we're not aware of it. Its objects, whether in the seventh century BC or the twenty-first century AD, will always fail. God hates it in His people now, even as He did in Isaiah's day. Idolatry destroys prayer and worship now as it did then. The Holy Spirit continues to expose this very serious sin.

One reason it was so difficult for the prophets to get the people to admit their idolatrous practices was because the people tried to mix worship of God with the worship of idols. For instance, when naming their children, parents would often give names borrowed from both the worship of God and the worship of Baal. In the Jerusalem Temple, King Manasseh overtly combined worship of God with worship of pagan deities.

God would not permit mixing worship of Him with that of pagan deities. The prophets warned that prayers offered in such a confused environment would completely fail and that the gods they had mixed together would fail. God would not share His glory with idols. The people couldn't see it (Jer. 2:4–13). They had exchanged the glory of God for something that has no profit (v.11).

What the prophets said in the Old Testament is true for us today. Are we prepared to recognise when we offer our prayers to gods that fail? Are we capable of seeing instances in which we have tried to mix worship of God with worship of 'gods'? Might we dig around a little in our prayers, public and private, to detect what the prophets might see?

The Holy Spirit works to keep things in order in the Church. For example, He distributes the gifts Christ has provided. He also exposes points at which we Christians have elevated finite interests to places of ultimate importance. *He will show where we have given to created things honour that belongs to God alone*. We should pray daily for the Holy Spirit to perform this work in Christ's Church and in us. At the most intense level, this is what revival means.

Often in the Church's history, the Holy Spirit has shaken everything that can be shaken so that all that cannot be shaken may remain (Heb. 12:27). For example, He shook the Church in the sixteenth century so that it could rediscover that fact that we are reconciled to God by grace through faith alone.

A LOT OF SHAKING GOING ON

With the Spirit's guidance, let's look for some of the gods we might have tried to mix with the worship of God. Let's invite the Holy Spirit to do some shaking and expose some of our prayers to 'gods'. Who knows? We might find some scarecrows in the cucumber field. Let's examine seven of the more prominent gods that plague popular Christianity.

The god of self

One god is the self-centred content of many of our prayers. Much prayer pivots around ourselves rather than being offered in worship of God and on behalf of others.

Our age has been correctly described as narcissistic. This exaggerated self-love and self-centredness is idolatrous and eventually destroys its host. If we pray as if we're the centre of the universe with our interests as God's chief concern, we create a god that needs to fail. God is concerned about each of us and about our needs. But a Christian's first and controlling interest should be the kingdom of God, which Jesus inaugurated. Christian prayer begins and ends in worship and adoration. It starts by saying, *Holy is Your name. Your will be done. Your kingdom come.* Only after that and in that spirit may we then say, *Give us this day ...*

The narcissistic distortion of popular Christianity has hindered worship of God and Christian community. When a person is narcissistic, other people come second. They may even become tools we can use for our own interests and aspirations. But when Jesus summarised the Law, He said, '"Love the Lord your God with all your heart and with all your soul and with all your mind." This is the first and greatest commandment. And the second is like it: "Love your neighbour as yourself"' (Matt. 22:37–39).

We do not need to go far to hear the god of narcissism. Listen to some preachers. Listen to our 'prayer requests'. Look at the thrust of some of our popular Christian books. Our pagan culture also primes the pump through advertising, television programming and films. Our culture provides ample temptations and opportunities to create and worship a god that is really simply an extension of ourselves.

Eventually this god will fail. For prayer to be truly Christian and received by the living God, we must let the Holy Spirit expose this god in the Church and in those of us who are members of Christ's Body. This will not be easy, for the error is deeply embedded in some of us.

The god of happiness

A second god that needs to fail is the god of happiness. Many of us live with an unending message that the chief end of life is to be happy and comfortable. The language imbeds itself into our Christian language, worship, expectations and self-understanding. Many of us have been tricked into thinking that achieving happiness is a primary Christian enterprise. It isn't.

Happiness relies heavily on surrounding circumstances. Our culture craves happiness and works around the clock to market all the supports necessary to make and keep us happy. The products come in bottles, pills, food and on wheels, wings and skis. Happiness arrives in the form of money, health, possessions, friends, leisure and more.

However, because the external conditions upon which happiness depends often change, happiness remains only as long as pleasant conditions persist. Don't worry, though – advertising will be there to offer another product.

Perhaps some of us will be surprised to learn that happiness isn't a principal interest of the Christian gospel or of the New Testament. It isn't mentioned as a Christian pursuit or virtue. If happiness were a primary Christian goal, Jesus would not have gone to the cross. Stephen would have averted being stoned to death and Paul would not have spent so much time in Roman prisons.

If happiness should not be a principal Christian pursuit, what should take its place? The New Testament answer is *joy* – joy in the Holy Spirit. Jesus hoped His joy would remain in the disciples and that their joy might be complete (John 15:11; 17:13). Paul prayed for the Roman Christians, 'May the God of hope fill you with all joy and peace in believing, so that you may abound in hope by the power of the Holy Spirit' (Rom. 15:13, NRSV).

This central Christian theme repeatedly rings out in the Gospels and epistles. The resurrection of Jesus Christ and the gift of the Holy Spirit are the source and guarantee of joy.

Those who firmly believe the message of the New Testament are convinced that joy has nothing to do with surrounding circumstances. It has everything to do with Christian hope and the peace of Christ. Who would long more for happiness when Christ's gift is joy? The apostle Paul said the essence of God's kingdom is not food and drink, but righteousness and peace and joy in the Holy Spirit (Rom. 14:17).

The Jewish and Roman authorities, jails, shipwrecks and violent mobs, gave Paul ample opportunity to prove that he believed this. He told the Philippian Christians about his joy in the Lord: 'I have learned to be content with whatever I have. I know what it is to have little, and I know what it is to have plenty ... I can do all things through him who strengthens me' (Phil. 4:11–13, NRSV). This is the fruit and evidence of Christian joy.

Now, let's admit it: we all want to be happy. We enjoy basic comforts and try to obtain them. But interest in happiness is not the issue. Turning it into a god and identifying this god with the God who inhabits eternity is the issue.

The god of happiness whom our culture worships is not

the god Christians should pray to. That pagan god must die, must be crucified by the crucified and resurrected Lord. The god of happiness is eating at the Church's life. But it will not die easily. It has been baptised and holds a certificate of church membership.

The god of blessings

The third god that must fail is the pervasive notion that material and physical blessings are chief evidences of God's presence and the primary goal of our faith. This god takes some cross forms. But it can also subtly creep into the Church. It is present as an idol when we evaluate people and give them positions in the Church based on what they own or their position in society.

James dealt forcefully with this idol: 'Brothers, as believers in our glorious Lord Jesus Christ, don't show favouritism ... Has not God chosen those who are poor in the eyes of the world to be rich in faith and to inherit the kingdom he promised those who love him?' (James 2:1, 5). We may know this false god is present whenever we assess a church's 'success' in quantifiable terms.

Never in human history has a culture been more material-istic than we are. Materialism claims that the most real and the most valuable elements are the material and the physical. 'Real' has become what a person can wear, hold, count, bank or sell.

Jesus and His disciples watched people place their offerings into the Temple treasury. The things that impressed the disciples most might also have impressed us, such as the Temple's grandeur. But they overlooked the widow who placed in the treasury the little she had.

Jesus left no doubt about the idol of materialism. Beginning with the Beatitudes in the Sermon on the Mount and extending to the Suffering Servant on the cross, He judged the god called materialism to be a child of hell and a sworn enemy of the cross. If the One beside whom there is none other is to be the centre of our worship and the goal of our prayers, the god named materialism must *fail* in us and in the Church.

The god of justice-free faith

The fourth god that the Holy Spirit wants to expose as an idol is the notion that we can love God without acting justly and showing loving-kindness. The belief that salvation is a private contract that can be signed, sealed and delivered apart from our neighbour, is rampant in popular Christianity. Hell would like nothing more than a salvation that doesn't include the neighbour, that doesn't require justice and loving-kindness.

In many instances, hell will get its wish, for a salvation is being offered that does not challenge racism, class consciousness, gender prejudice, illiteracy and economic exploitation.

The prophets Amos and Micah blasted all forms of religion that let people 'fix things with God' without paying attention to justice. 'Take away the noise of your songs,' God told Israel. 'But let justice roll down like waters, and righteousness like an ever-flowing stream' (Amos 5:23–24, NRSV).

Through Jeremiah, God asked the people of Judah, 'Is not this to know me – to do justice and righteousness and to [judge] the cause of the poor and needy?' (See Jer. 22:15–17, NRSV).

Do we remember those whom the Son of Man says will inherit the kingdom of God? They are the ones to whom He can say, 'For I was hungry and you gave me something to eat, I was thirsty and you gave me something to drink, I was a stranger and you invited me in, I needed clothes and you clothed me, I was sick and you looked after me, I was in prison and you came to visit me' (Matt. 25:35–36).

The gospel of Jesus Christ is nothing apart from the kingdom of God. The gospel is the gospel of the kingdom. No one receives the gospel unless he or she recognises that the long-expected kingdom of God has come in Jesus of Nazareth. This is the good news that calls all people to repent and to receive the kingdom. But to receive the kingdom is to see and believe that the old order of sin, hatred, injustice, violence and exploitation has been, and is being, judged and condemned. The old order is passing away and the new has come. This requires a radical reorientation of a person's entire life and interests, not just a private salvation contract that leaves out the kingdom of God that has come to earth and will come in its fullness.

All prayer to God offered in the name of a god that forsakes justice and mercy is idolatrous. It will and should fail.

The god of village deities
Another god that will and must fail is the insidious practice of limiting the range of God's interest and care to our own nation, family, race, denomination and class. This is the sin that the people of Judah committed when they believed that God's life depended on the Temple's existence. *No Temple, no God*, they thought. *So God will have to protect the Temple and Jerusalem to save Himself.*

We should know better, but when many of us pray – publicly or privately – God seems to be no larger than the 'half a log' taken from the forest (Isa. 44:19) and, not surprisingly, the 'half a log' god looks a lot like us.

For some of us, our god has become just one more village deity, as is worshipped in many parts of the world. Judging by the words some of us pray, God certainly doesn't sound like the Creator and sustainer of the universe. He doesn't sound like the Lord of all, the Holy One. He doesn't sound like the One who was before all things, and in whom all things now hold together (Col. 1:17). In some Christian circles, God seems to have been turned into a localised deity who needs to be transported from place to place and nailed down so he won't topple over. He is then instructed to endorse and bless one petty interest after another.

The Holy Spirit works diligently to set us free from village deities. Through the resurrection of Jesus and through Pentecost, the Holy Spirit has exploded the notion that God is like other gods that limit their interests and power to the tribes that worship them. When, on the Day of Pentecost, the Holy Spirit made it possible for all those present to hear the good news in their own languages, God sent a clear message that His kingdom and reign are universal (Acts 2:1–4). The same was true when the Lord sent Peter to Cornelius's house (Acts 10).

Prayer that is Christian and free from gods will recognise that the holy and loving God sends rain on the just and the unjust (Matt. 5:45). He is the missionary God, who longs that no one perish but that all people everywhere come to eternal life (John 3:16). As Peter learned on the rooftop in Joppa, efforts to transport tribal deities into the kingdom of the gospel will utterly fail (Acts 10:9–16). Our prayers must show that we know this.

The god of proof

The sixth highly influential and guaranteed-to-fail god among some Christians is the pagan practice of putting God to the test. Somewhere close to the centre of what sin means is the practice of setting conditions by which God can prove

He is God. The tempter has no greater ploy than to deceive Christians into thinking that telling God how to be God is actually an expression of faith.

Satan used this approach to tempt Jesus. In so many words, he said, 'Let's see whether or not you really are the Son of God. Jump off the pinnacle of the Temple. If God sends angels to catch you, then we'll know.'

Was the tempter urging Jesus to place His faith in His heavenly Father? No, not at all. He simply wanted Him to call the shots, deciding the terms by which God could prove Himself.

Throughout Jesus' ministry on earth some people continued to ask for another miracle or sign. They said, 'Hey, Jesus – we don't yet believe. But we'll give you another chance to convince us. Give us just one more sign or miracle, and we'll come on board.' Jesus never fell for that trap. He knew that putting God to the test would never lead to radical trust in God alone.

Those who try to set the conditions under which God can be God want to put Him on a short leash. He'll never do enough for them, for their desire to control springs straight from hell. It springs straight out of the unbelief that emptied heaven of the devil and his allies and drove Adam and Eve from the Garden of Eden.

In Gethsemane, Jesus forever put the lid on testing the Father: 'My Father, if it is possible, may this cup be taken from me. Yet not as I will, but as you will' (Matt. 26:39). By contrast, the 'god of testing' plagues popular Christianity. In prayers, sermons, books and songs, this god presents itself as Christian faith. Many try to incorporate this idol into their worship of God. The two will never successfully mix, no matter how many false prophets declare it possible.

The warning against 'testing' God should not be confused

with presenting our petitions to the Lord. The Lord urges His children to present their petitions to their heavenly Father. We do so in faith and worship. We wait patiently to see how God will reveal His aid. The warning is against turning petitions into conditions that God must meet before we will worship and have faith in Him.

Perhaps this is a good time to return to Habakkuk. When we left him in Chapter 1, he was in a serious religious funk. He was mad at God and wanted everyone to know it. His god had failed.

In the second chapter of Habakkuk, God tells Habakkuk that those who live as God's friends will live by faith. They will not place their trust in idols, kings and armies. They will not assess God's faithfulness on every contrary wind that blows. Their trust will be anchored in God's character and His long record of faithfulness to Himself and His people (2:4).

Well, the message got through to Habakkuk. I think that no words in all the Old Testament – perhaps even the New Testament – surpass Habakkuk's affirmation of radical faith in God. He has finished 'testing' and judging God. He is done with the god of happiness and all tribal deities. Listen to his hymn of radical faith:

> Though the fig tree does not blossom,
>   and no fruit is on the vines;
> though the produce of the olive fails
>   and the fields yield no food;
> though the flock is cut off from the fold
>   and there is no herd in the stalls,
> yet I will rejoice in the LORD;
>   I will exult in the God of my salvation.
> GOD, the Lord, is my strength ... (3:17–19, NRSV)

04

In defence of a faith that doubts

'I BELIEVE;
HELP MY UNBELIEF'

If the New Testament seems clear about anything, it's that prayer and faith cannot live peaceably in the same house with doubt. Jesus told us, 'Have faith in God. Truly I tell you, if you say to this mountain, "Be taken up and thrown into the sea," and if you do not doubt in your heart, but believe that what you say will come to pass, it will be done for you' (Mark 11:22–23, NRSV).

But is it not possible that *doubt*, at least one form of it, has an unfair reputation? I think so, and I believe that unless we defend this doubt, we will mistreat many of Jesus' disciples.

My model for this chapter is an unnamed father who appears briefly in Mark 9:14–29 (see also Matt. 17:14–21; Luke 9:37–42). Driven to frustration by seizures ravaging his epileptic son, the father brought the child to Jesus. The dad had already appealed to the disciples, who couldn't help. So he implored Jesus to have pity on his son. Jesus said, 'Bring him to me', and told the man that if he would believe, the child would be healed.

Perhaps, given the man's desperation, we could have expected a glowing, unambiguous affirmation of faith. Instead, in transparent honesty the man cried, 'I believe; help my unbelief!' (Mark 9:24, NRSV).

How did Jesus respond? Did he say, 'I'm sorry. That isn't good enough. When you can believe without reservation, bring the boy back'?

Absolutely not. Jesus heard the father's anguished cry, looked into his heart, and healed the boy. Matthew says the boy 'was healed from that moment' (17:18).

The father's honest response opens a door for many of Jesus' disciples whose life experiences place them in that father's company. Almost instinctively they understand his cry. For some, the father's appeal to Jesus may be contradictory. They would say that a person either has faith or does not. Either a person believes or he or she does not. Faithful doubt? Impossible. Defensible or not, Jesus healed the child.

The best response to the father's anguished appeal is not logic or argument, but life – an honest report on both faith and life. If doubt – even serious doubt – and the prayer of faith are mutually exclusive, then lop off a good portion of the Church. Let it then be composed only of Christians who have never, with broken hearts and trembling lips, uttered such words as the father's.

Annie Dillard's *Pilgrim at Tinker Creek* is a rich portrayal of nature's beauty and complexity. But the book can be deceptive. Dillard's underlying agenda is to struggle with some of the plaguing questions that confront people of faith. She wrestles with the mixed signals about God that nature gives us.

At one point she describes frogs jumping along Tinker Creek in the summer. At first the scene invites one to think innocently about nature. Dillard describes the rich green grass in which the frogs were playing. The jumping and croaking of the creatures thrilled her.

Then Dillard saw a frog lying still, partly in and partly out of the water. Presently, it slowly crumpled and began to sag. The spirit disappeared from its eyes. The frog shrank. Like 'a deflating football', the tight, glistening skin on the frog's shoulders rumpled and fell. 'Soon, part of his skin, formless as a pricked balloon, lay in floating folds like bright scum on top of the water.' It was, Dillard wrote, monstrous and terrifying. She says she 'gaped bewildered, appalled'.[1]

What had happened to the glistening frog? A giant water bug had eaten it by sucking out the frog's insides. It could do the same to fish and tadpoles.

For many Christians, crises in life have drained energies and faith even as the water bug drained the frog. Examined on the surface, they appear to have things under control. But beneath the surface they're nearly immobilised by personal, family, emotional or professional failures. Their eyes dulled, their faith rumpled, they've all but collapsed like the frog in Tinker Creek.

These people may be the loneliest people in Christ's Church. In the words of the captain in the film *Cool Hand Luke*, these Christians might say to God, 'What we've got here is failure to communicate.' There doesn't seem to be much of a place for them or much that can be said for them. We don't want to parade them in city-wide crusades. They would ruin praise gatherings. Why, they can't even lift their hands when choruses are sung. And you won't find their pictures on brochures that advertise success seminars. Maybe they're better off left in the shadows where they can't discourage others.

If this is true, the gospel of Jesus Christ is a hoax that should be publicly exposed. If this is how we should treat the 'faithful doubter', what are we to make of Jesus' invitation, 'Come to me, all you who are weary and burdened, and I will give you rest. Take my yoke upon you and learn from me, for I am gentle and humble in heart, and you will find rest for your souls. For my yoke is easy and my burden is light' (Matt. 11:28–29).

TWO KINDS OF DOUBT

At least two kinds of doubt exist. One is the doubt of a rebel. The other is that of a child of God. The two kinds of doubt should not be confused. The doubt of the rebel is born of *unfaith*. The doubt of the child of God is born of *faith*.

The *first* kind of doubt shouts, 'No God for me!' It's the parent of sin. This form of doubt wants to put distance between the rebel and God. The rebel neither believes that God 'is' nor that God should be the Lord of all.

In the mood of much modern atheism, rebellious doubt says, 'No one is here but us, thank you, and we want to keep it that way.' God is chased out of the world. 'God' is a concept to be opposed, the rebel says, in the interest of human freedom. A long list of nineteeth- and twentieth-century figures belongs to this fraternity, which includes some sophisticated intellectuals and gurus of popular culture.

The doubt of the rebel has nothing in common with the cry of the father of the epileptic child.

The *second* kind of doubt, that of the child of God, may at first seem strange. Whereas the doubt of the rebel springs from unbelief, the doubt of the child of God springs from faith. 'Lord, I believe', is its first movement, however faint and undetectable it might be. More correctly, the doubt of the child of God is actually an affirmation of faith. It is doubt that 'doubts' in the name of faith. It banks on belief. It springs from a longing for God to show Himself to be exactly who He says He is.

Maybe in tones subdued by tragedy, perhaps in reaction to disappointments associated with prayer and faith, or maybe in bitter anger and protest, 'faithful doubt' calls out for God's faithfulness.

LAMENTS IN THE OLD TESTAMENT

Faithful doubt is born from a discrepancy between what the doubter believes about God's faithfulness and goodness, and what he or she has actually observed in life. In the Old Testament this kind of doubt is called a 'lament'.

The Hebrews gave a lot of space in the Scriptures for laments. Their life with God in a complex and often hostile world demanded it. Faithfulness to the tension between living in faithful obedience to God even while experiencing life's harsh realities, often gave birth to lament. The Hebrews included laments in the hymnody they used in worship. Laments fill one-third of the Psalms. In unmistakable language, laments arise from 'out of the depths' (Psa. 130:1). In richly diverse language, laments cry out, 'Lord, we believe; help thou our unbelief.'

The Old Testament contains laments of the *community* (Psa. 10; 74; 79; 105; 137) and of *individuals* (Psa. 3; 13; 22; 31; 54; 56; 102). They are lasting and instructive expressions of 'faithful doubt'.

Sometimes, when the community or individuals re-membered God's deeds of deliverance in the past and contrasted them with their present situation of suffering and distress, the result often plunged 'an individual or the whole Israelite community into bewilderment'.[2]

Sometimes Israel felt as though God had abandoned His people. But self-pity or vindictive bitterness never characterises the laments. The laments honestly reveal this. But they never display abandonment of faith or vindictive bitterness against God. Even amid lament, the lament psalms also contain faith and praise. The laments are actually expressions of 'faithful' or 'worshipful' doubt!

Sometimes the righteous passionately cry out for God's vindication against the wicked. The wicked have mockingly asked the righteous, 'Where is your God?' (Psa. 7; 17; 26). In great penitential psalms, the cry 'from the depths' comes from those who have plumbed the human problem at its deepest level. The speaker knows no solution to the human predicament exists apart from divine forgiveness (Psa. 51; 130):

> If you, O LORD, kept a record of sins,
>> O Lord, who could stand?
> But with you there is forgiveness;
>> therefore you are feared. (Psa. 130:3–4)

JESUS' LAMENT AND OURS

But that's the Old Testament. Is there any place for laments in the New Testament? Shouldn't the Christian faith be characterised by the gospel's good news and the Holy Spirit's abiding presence? Living in the joy of the Holy Spirit, shouldn't Christians always be able to express victory and confidence?

Not so fast. Do the following words sound familiar? 'My

God, my God, why have you forsaken me?' (Mark 15:34; Matt. 27:46). They are the anguished words of Jesus from the cross, which sprung from 'out of the depths'. They are also words from Psalm 22:1, an Old Testament lament: 'My God, my God, why have you forsaken me? Why are you so far from helping me, from the words of my groaning?' Jesus used the lament to voice His own question.

Was Jesus engaged in charades, or was He actually expressing anguished 'faithful doubt' from His own 'depths'?

It is sometimes difficult for us to believe that Jesus was really tempted in all points, even as we are. But His words on the cross grandly testify to the fact. The event of the cross was no divine game staged to impress the Jews and Jesus' disciples. There God took upon Himself the abyss, the bottom depths, of human suffering, sin and abandonment.

Jesus' lament can help us better understand the Incarnation. In Him God really did become one with us. He really did bear our burdens, even the burden of 'faithful doubt'. The Son of God took upon Himself the form of a servant and became obedient to the point of death (Phil. 2:1–11).

Jesus' words on the cross forever answer the question of whether a child of God can legitimately express 'faithful doubt'. Jesus cried out, 'Why have you forsaken me?'. Therefore, all of God's children can cry from their own depths and from the depths of those for whom they intercede – those who may not even be able to pray for themselves.

It is important to add that Jesus' lament, like all true faithful doubt, is actually an expression of profound faith in God. Like the psalmist in Psalm 22, Jesus was confidently calling upon His heavenly Father to be as faithful as Jesus believed Him to be. 'My God, My God' means 'Be faithful to Yourself, O Lord'; or 'Be who I believe You are'.

So, as strange as it may seem, Jesus' lament from out of the depths was an expression of praise. Before His resurrection, while still in the depths, Jesus affirmed that His Father would show His strong arm of redemption. Psalm 22, from which He was quoting, concludes, 'From you comes the theme of my praise in the great assembly ... for dominion belongs to the LORD and he rules over the nations' (Psa. 22:25, 28).

When did God confirm the Son's praise and confidence? It happened on Easter morning, when the angel rolled away the stone from the grave. The New Testament tells us that God, by His power, raised Jesus from the grave (Rom. 6:4; Col. 2:12).

The New Testament also tells us that as Jesus' disciples, we, too, partake in His resurrection. The same God of power who raised Jesus from the grave, now, by the Holy Spirit, works in us (2 Cor. 13:4; Eph. 1:15–23). Even in the face of 'faithful doubt' we are made alive through Christ Jesus our Lord.

What should be done with the faithful doubters among us, those who are brothers and sisters to the epileptic child's father? Should we be dismissed from the Church as an embarrassment to people who possess a sparkling, confident faith? Maybe *we* should just be abandoned and they hope *we* go away. Just shuffle *us* off to the edge as second-class residents in the household of God.

My friend Vicki asks, 'If those who doubt as God's children get shuffled to the edge in the Church, how will sinners ever find their way home?'

Vicki tells of an alcoholic in her Maryland town who stumbled into church 'drunker than a skunk'. 'With remnants of a voice once beautiful, Jake sang with the rest of us "on a hill far away stood an old rugged cross". But the congregation thought Jake and his singing were quite out of place.' Vicki concludes, 'Jake never came back.'

Abandon them? Never. As long as Jesus Christ is the Saviour and friend of the weary, and as long as He is the One the Father raised from the grave on Easter morning, God will never abandon the faithful doubters.

The One who voiced His own lament on the cross, who was dead and buried, and who was raised by God's power, calls the 'faithful doubters' His sisters and brothers. No one can change that, not even hell! Nothing 'will be able to separate us from the love of God that is in Christ Jesus our Lord' (Rom. 8:39).

When 'faithful doubters' pray, their prayers may not sound like models of confidence and victory. For those who think that doubt and faith are incompatible, the prayers of the 'faithful doubters' may be offensive or embarrassing. Speaking for himself, a friend who is no beginner in the Christian faith told me, 'The dark night of the soul is the way of life for some.'

If the record of God's people in the Bible and in the Church is true, if God's character as disclosed in the Scriptures is dependable, then the prayers of the 'faithful doubters' express faith as surely as any other prayers. As anguished and shaky as these prayers may be, they come from God's children and are directed to Him. He receives them and responds with His steadfast, inseparable love.

05

Tragedy and the Christian life

'AH BARTLEBY!
AH, HUMANITY!'

One of the most puzzling stories in American literature is 'Bartleby the Scrivener',[1] which Herman Melville wrote in 1853. The main character, Bartleby, copied legal documents in the New York office of the Mastery in Chancery.

At first Bartleby worked very hard. His employer would have been quite pleased with his work had Bartleby been 'cheerfully industrious. But he wrote on silently, palely, mechanically.'

Then things changed sharply. Part of Bartleby's assignment was to proofread the work of the attorney and the other copyists. One day the attorney wanted Bartleby to help him examine a small document, expecting immediate compliance.

Bartleby responded, 'I would prefer not to.'

From that day, in spite of threats, enticements and questioning, 'I would prefer not to' was all Bartleby ever said. He never explained why he abruptly stopped working. Much of the rest of the story traces the attorney's efforts either to motivate Bartleby, dismiss him or to get away from him.

Eventually Bartleby became a vagrant, and the police moved him to the Tombs – a combination of prison, asylum and place for the poor. Bartleby refused to eat and finally died of starvation.

Near the end of the story we don't know any more than we did at the beginning. Why did Bartleby suddenly 'prefer not to'? The answer is in the story's short sequel. *Bartleby had been immobilised by the depth and magnitude of human tragedy.*

Before becoming a scrivener, Bartleby had been a clerk in the Dead Letter Office in Washington, DC, where he had sorted undeliverable letters and burned them by the cartload.

Sometimes from out of a folded paper Bartleby would retrieve a ring. The finger for which it was meant perhaps now rotted in the grave. From another letter Bartleby might pull a bank note sent to address a desperate need for charity. But perhaps because of a faulty address, the urgently needed relief never reached the intended recipient. Other letters included forgiveness for those who died not knowing they had been forgiven. Good tidings were there for people who might have died in despair because the good news didn't reach them.

Bartleby had seen all of this in the Dead Letter Office. Confronting so much human pain and tragedy finally overcame him. Working feverishly, he had tried to avoid his confrontation with tragedy. He had not succeeded. Tragedy caught up with him in the attorney's office. Bartleby faced the futility of endlessly copying legal documents.

What am I to make of a world where even when people try to do good, despair and disappointment often result? he must have asked himself. He decided that continuing to copy documents was an insult to those who suffer tragedy. The world, he concluded, with all its hectic activities is finally a dead letter office. Only the blind can't see it. Continue to copy? He would 'prefer not to'.

We will probably agree that Bartleby's analysis of the human situation was too extreme. But no one who has struggled with some of life's senseless and tragic experiences will quickly dismiss what Bartleby had observed.

Humanity has wrestled with the reality of tragedy at least since the time of the early Greeks in the fifth century BC. No one can give a single sufficient definition of tragedy. We associate efforts to understand it with Greeks such as Euripides, Sophocles and Aristotle; with the German Goethe; the Englishmen William Shakespeare, Samuel Johnson and Thomas Hardy; and with the Russian Fyodor Dostoyevsky.

CHRISTIANS AND TRAGEDY

Tragedy often invades the lives of Christians. We're no more immune than anyone else. Some Christians seem to expect faith and tragedy to exclude each other. Not so.

Many of us know this from experience. A Pollyanna approach that tries to avoid an honest response to tragedy is sub-Christian. Failure to confront tragedy honestly can compound the sufferings of those who endure it. The Christian faith provides a better response to tragedy than avoidance or denial. It meets tragedy head-on and ultimately meets it with redemption.

What is tragedy? No uniform definition exists. The Greeks largely thought of it as an inherent weakness in a hero that would finally bring him down. The defeat would spring from an unforeseen and unavoidable failure.

But the Greek way isn't the only way to understand tragedy. Tragedy also includes the unexpected occurrence of things in life that are, or become, badly broken through no direct fault of the one on whom tragedy falls. There was probably no realistic way to have anticipated or avoided the failure. Tragedy always frustrates potential, hopes and goals in unexpected ways. It is the evil that results from what we cannot control and for which no blame should be assigned. It comes from a collision of circumstances and factors that are beyond human management – at least beyond management by the one who suffers tragedy. People who suffer tragedy are usually keenly and painfully alert to their predicament.

Tragedy can result from inescapable conflict that obstructs community and peace. Nineteenth-century German writer Goethe said that all tragedy depends on insoluble conflict. It thrives in the womb of contradictions. As soon as harmony arrives, tragedy ceases. Tragedy includes the painful and harmful, even crippling, life experiences that result even though people have tried to do what they thought was right. It results not from vice or depravity but from error, frailty and even ignorance. Without warning, it can unleash suffering, confusion and even despair into our lives.

In some instances, tragedy can be overcome and undone in this life. In other instances it cannot. A person caught in tragedy can't just will his or her way out of it. Tragedy shows us just how vulnerable human life is. All of us are subject to it, regardless of our strengths.

Tragedy does seem to be a difficult reality for many Christians to confront or explain. We know how to deal with *sin* (rebellion against God and His righteous rule) because we know the meaning and importance of rebellion, faithlessness, repentance, redemption and restoration. We seem to know what to say about *righteousness* because we know the meaning of justification and sanctification. So we tend to apply those two words to all of life's experiences.

Usually, unless we're speaking of natural evil such as the devastation a hurricane causes, we tend to equate *sin* with *evil*. If we can't find an immediate guilty party on which to hang the word *sin*, we can at least work back to 'the Fall' to find one. Eventually, that's where Christians must land in their explanations of evil. But if we run there too quickly, we will mistakenly assign 'blameworthiness' (guilt) to things for which no blame is due.

Bad things happen to people to whom the word *guilt* doesn't apply. If we assign blame or guilt in all instances, we add undeserved suffering to people facing maddening situations. Many people suffer when no blame is due. Nevertheless, the suffering can almost strip life from them.

Evil is bigger than sin. If the gospel is as true and comprehensive of life as we claim, it must make a place for destructive experiences in life that cannot be labelled 'sin'. We must find better ways to voice the gospel to people who live with uninvited sorrows, failures and sufferings. People who live under these oppressions know them to be evil. But they also know they have not rebelled against God.

One day Jesus and His disciples saw a man who had been blind since birth. The disciples explained the man's plight by assuming that either the man or his parents had sinned. So they asked Jesus, 'Rabbi, who sinned, this man or his parents?' Jesus answered them, 'Neither' (John 9:1–3).

THEIR STORIES

Stan. Four years out of Bible college, Stan and his wife, Virginia, were doing well in their first pastoral assignment. They were much respected in their small community, especially by the young people. Stan and Virginia had started a Saturday night coffeehouse ministry for teenagers in the community. The congregation had bought a used bus for transporting children to Sunday School and for taking teenagers to various events.

Early on a Monday morning in July, Stan and a group of teenagers, including some whose parents did not come to church, were to leave for a week of summer camp. As usual, some were late. So the bus pulled out of the church car park over one hour later than scheduled.

Stan and the noisy bunch of teenagers were not more than a mile from the church when he prepared to cross the railway line he had crossed in the bus many times. Vision at the crossing was partly obscured by an embankment. With a high noise level in the bus, Stan approached the crossing. From the corner of his eye he saw a train approaching. He braked hard, but the brake booster failed. His legs were not strong enough to stop the bus in time. The train slammed into the front of the bus and dragged it more than 60 metres before throwing it free.

When the bus came to a stop it was on its side and badly damaged. Most of the youngsters survived with minor-to-moderate injuries. But not 16-year-old Laura, who had recently begun attending the church. Laura's neck had broken, and she died. Stan was devastated. He had set out to take a group of teenagers to a place where they could grow in their faith, have a week of good fellowship and hear the gospel preached. Now one of them was dead.

Laura's mother did not attend Stan's church. Her grief was deep and understandable. She refused to believe Stan's account of the accident. She hired a lawyer and sued Stan and the church for negligence.

In court Stan could not convince the jurors that the brakes had momentarily failed. The judgment went strongly against him and the church. To make matters worse, some local people and church members turned against him. He was judged a careless culprit.

Stan and Virginia never recovered from Laura's death, the senselessness of the accident and the venom directed at Stan. He had no way to vindicate himself and was never invited to re-establish ministry in another congregation. All that happened 15 years ago.

For 15 years now, Stan and Virginia have lived with the grief, shame and suffering generated by the accident, trial and the end of their ministry. Stan and Virginia personify tragedy.

Deborah. Never did a more chaste person enter a Christian college than Deborah. Bright, disciplined and focused, she knew why she was there. Even as a child in a small rural church, Deborah knew God had called her to be a missionary nurse. Though her parents could not provide much financial help, she completed her college and registered nurse training in only five years – at the top of her class.

While in college, Deborah fell in love with one of the most promising students on campus, whom God had also called to become a missionary. The two of them served effectively for years in Latin America. They had two children. Deborah could have written a book on how wonderfully God leads. She used her own obedience to God for instructing young people.

In time Deborah and her husband returned to the United States, where her husband pastored a prominent congregation. After a few years of effective ministry, Deborah's husband resigned. Weeks later, out of nowhere, Deborah's husband told her that he was homosexual and had been all his life. Deborah was shattered. She tried every redemptive strategy she could imagine. But everything failed.

Today Deborah lives alone. Her husband remains in the homosexual community. What did Deborah do wrong? Did she miss God's will while in college? Did she disobey God by marrying someone who shared her call to missions?

Nothing could lead us to place blame on Deborah. She believed she was succeeding. Then, while in early middle age, her world fell apart. Tragedy, not normality, became her daily companion. Try as she might, Deborah has not been able to fix what was broken. Given the long incubation period of the HIV virus, Deborah knows the danger she faces in the future.

Richard and Marjorie. The year was 1971. Richard and Marjorie Brown had spent their lives preparing to serve as doctors in a rural area. They knew this was what God wanted, and they were willing to do it. After years of medical school and residency, they were ready to move to their new home. A small town had built a small clinic for them.

As Richard and Marjorie prepared to move, they learned that both of their sons, aged six and eight, had sickle cell disease, a red blood cell disorder inherited from parents. In the United States one out of every ten African Americans is a carrier. One out of every four hundred black people has the disease. In 1971 the disease gained the attention of the medical community. Through screening, the disease had been detected in both of Marjorie and Richard's sons.

In sickle cell disease, complications include pain episodes, strokes, infections, leg ulcers, bone damage, yellow eyes or jaundice, early gallstones, lung blockage, kidney damage and more. The progression of the disease is punctuated by crises with fever and attacks of pain in the arms, legs, heart or abdomen. It is incurable.

To care for the boys' needs as the disease progressed, Marjorie and Richard had to postpone their plans. Later the plans were cancelled altogether. Eddie, the younger son, died in 1982. Josh, the older boy, died in 1984. The final years for both sons were extremely difficult.

Emotionally and psychologically, Marjorie did not survive. She has barely survived spiritually. Effective prayers escaped her some years ago. The best she can now do is mumble a few nearly incoherent sentences that we might call prayer.

Richard keeps a relatively successful medical practice going in Nebraska. He has maintained greater resolve and stability as a Christian than Marjorie. He teaches an adult Sunday School class. But he has never overcome the pain and confusion associated with having to abandon the service he believed God had designed for him.

THE GOSPEL AND TRAGEDY

What good word can the gospel of Jesus Christ offer to those who live with tragedy? Does the gospel have a place for them? Or does the gospel tell them, 'When you get your house in order, call again'? How are people who live in tragic conditions supposed to pray? Living daily in a tragic setting can limit or even suffocate prayer.

Can the gospel include the reality of tragedy in its provision for human life? Is the gospel that large? Some Christians don't think so. They believe tragedy belongs only to a pagan world-view. I believe an adequate gospel will include in its provision all people who know the reality of tragedy. It doesn't leave them out.

But the gospel and a totally tragic view of the world *are incompatible*. Christian confidence is that when the kingdom of God is complete, God's peace will reign over all of God's creation. The Christian faith has no room for accepting tragedy as a permanent resident in God's creation. Tragedy has a limited life span. The Christian confidence is that 'God will wipe away every tear' (Rev. 7:17). Evil of every kind has a termination date in God's scheme of redemption. The resurrection of Jesus guarantees it, and the Holy Spirit tells us to expect it.

But until the end comes and the Father has put all things under Christ's feet (1 Cor. 15:25), we must face the reality of tragedy in the world and in people's lives. It must not be written off with superficial solutions or dismissed through a careless use of the Scriptures.

For example, we too easily reach for Romans 8:28 as a catchall explanation for tragedy: '... we know that in all things God works for the good of those who love him, who have been called according to his purpose.' But we abuse the verse.

Sometimes we hear people say the verse means all the horrible things that happen to people finally turn out to be good. Others say that if people will just be patient, evil will pass away and the good will replace it. Another variation is that those who love the Lord will eventually see that all they thought was evil was in fact 'good in disguise'.

It is true that some things in life we thought were evil later turn out to be blessings in disguise. It is also true that, by God's grace, many harmful things that happen can be overcome and made to serve good purposes.

But Romans 8:28 does not say that in time all negative,

harmful and destructive occurrences in life will turn out to be good. The repeated sexual abuse of a child will never become good, no matter how much 'grace' is eventually applied. Only an insensitive person would ever tell the child that God meant the abuse for his or her good. Nor do we believe that as an adult, the sexually abused person will look back on the abuse as being a good thing. Sexual abuse of children is a destructive crime and will never be anything else. God has no interest in calling good what is in fact evil.

Rather than twisting texts in directions that help us transform the evil that ravages lives, Fredrick Buechner challenges Christians – particularly Christian ministers – to come to grips with tragedy and to find effective ways to apply the gospel to it. Beneath our religion, he says, 'we are all vulnerable to the storm without and to the storm within, and if ever we are to find true shelter, it is with the recognition of our tragic nakedness and need for true shelter that we have to start'.

More pointedly, to Christian ministers, Buechner says, 'This is also where anyone who preaches the gospel has to start.' We have not, Buechner says, fully preached the gospel when we address it only to problems that can be solved.

Romans 8:28 does teach us that no matter how bitter the memories, intense the evil or sharp the pain, the Redeemer God will work ceaselessly to achieve His good purposes in us, and that no evil can keep Him from accomplishing this. The creative work of our Redeemer does not eliminate or deny the evil that people have experienced. Instead, in the power of Christ's resurrection, God works to show that the New Creation will have the final say.

Confronting tragedy head-on, giving tragedy its full due, will require us to hold a realistic view of life. Buechner believes that no matter what the tragedy, God will perform His healing work in us. But, he cautions, the 'sheltering word' of hope and resurrection cannot be spoken unless we have also carefully listened, paid honest attention to tragedy. Our 'listening' to the tragic, he says, is also part of the 'Christian word' that we have to articulate.

The gospel of Christ doesn't close our ears or shield our eyes from tragedy. Instead, we're urged to listen to the anguish that tragedy unleashes in people, families and nations.

No one who has superficially dismissed tragedy can speak the gospel as 'good news' if he or she has refused to listen. 'Listening' in the name of the gospel will show that we also recognise when we're exposed, vulnerable and 'without a roof over our heads'. The 'answering word', Buechner says, comes 'only after the [listening] word'.

Buechner cautions Christian ministers about the pressure to speak only an 'answer' without first speaking 'the listening word'. He or she must listen deeply to the questions that tragedy asks. The preacher dare not yield to pressure if he or she is serious about preaching the whole gospel.[2]

What then is the 'answering word' of the gospel for those whom tragedy has ambushed?

Jesus gave it in the following words: 'Come to me, all you who are weary and burdened, and I will give you rest' (Matt. 11:28).

Jesus' invitation and promise are for all people. They are certainly for Christians who live under the weight of tragedy. Jesus doesn't promise that He'll fix everything, but that He'll give us rest. Short of the kingdom being completed, tragedy will continue to plague the lives of many of God's children. Realistically, in many instances the tragedy will not go away. Reconciliation, restoration of family, friendship, ministry and effective service just might not occur. Still, Jesus' promise remains, 'I will give you rest', even if the tragic exists.

The first nine Beatitudes also form part of the gospel's answering word to those living in the shadow of tragedy:

> Blessed are the poor in spirit, for theirs is the kingdom of heaven.
> Blessed are those who mourn, for they will be comforted.
> Blessed are the meek, for they will inherit the earth.
> Blessed are those who hunger and thirst for righteousness, for they will be filled.
> Blessed are the merciful, for they will be shown mercy.
> Blessed are the pure in heart, for they will see God.
> Blessed are the peacemakers, for they will be called sons of God. (Matt. 5:3–9)

TRAGEDY AND NATURE

Richard and Marjorie's tragic story points out a close connection between humans, nature and tragedy. Often we encounter tragedy because things that happen in nature radically interrupt our lives. Normally the interplay between people and the natural order promotes a fair measure of harmony.

However, in many instances, the relationship between the natural order and humanity takes a different direction – natural evil. Natural evil is the human suffering resulting from a clash between human well-being and the forces of nature.

The weather conditions that generate a hurricane are not evil. But when a killer hurricane roars through communities, lives are lost, sources of incomes destroyed and normal patterns of life harshly disrupted. And while natural evil creates an opportunity for people to express generosity, it also sets the conditions for elevated prices, looting, and greed.

Bill Comeau voiced his response to all this in poetry:

Can't you understand, Lord?
We just can't see where all this is taking us ...
All around us there are the nonsense happenings
That seem to persist day after day
Grating against all logic
Against all that would make sense.
And the world around us,
Your world without end we hope,
sinks slowly into confusion and fear.[3]

Christians account for the clashes between nature and people by saying nature is 'fallen'. We don't turn natural evils into deities that have to be placated by some sort of sacrifice. We know creation was created by, and belongs to, our heavenly Father, who is holy love.

By the 'fall' of nature we mean that the fall of humanity resulting from Adam and Eve's refusal to trust God in the Garden of Eden negatively affected the natural order as well as humans. It impacted the whole of creation.

We should not take this to mean that something is fundamentally wrong with the structure of the universe. A physicist or biologist entering the laboratory to conduct research depends on nature being 'in order'. If the natural order were in some way fallen, as humans are fallen, then the regularity in science that produces successful and beneficial research would cease.

So what do Christians mean when they speak of the 'fall of

nature'? First, we mean that even though nature acts according to fixed norms, immense destruction and suffering often results when humanity and nature get in each other's way.

Second, we also know that sinful humanity can, and has, forced nature to serve ends contrary to God's will. Such abuses also subvert human well-being. Using the force of gravity to speed a bullet on a murderous mission is one example. Use of the natural sciences to produce things that harm people is another.

We can see many examples of this in the past 200 years. Humans have found ways to kidnap and force almost every segment of the natural order into sin's service. Even things humans could not reach – such as the heavenly bodies – they have turned into 'gods' that supposedly hold power over them. Just look at the astrology column in the daily newspaper.

How does the Bible deal with this? Does it just write off nature as hopelessly evil? Is nature an evil shell in which the good spirit is imprisoned, awaiting its release? Did a good God create the soul or spirit and an evil god create the physical world? Various religions have embraced these options. The Bible rejects all of them.

The Bible teaches us that the holy and loving God created the world and called it good. Anyone who makes the world God's sworn opponent or who thinks it has been hijacked in some way so that God's will cannot be accomplished has already moved out of the Hebraic–Christian orbit. This error has happened many times in the Christian Church. And it haunts the pages of much current Christian literature.

Nevertheless, the Bible does confront the sometimes tragic conflict between humans and nature. This tension shows up early in the biblical record. Genesis 3:16–19 should be read in this light. But the Bible also teaches that this warp in God's creation will not be permanent. Both the Old and New Testaments look forward to a time when the tragic quality of nature, and humanity's relationship to it, will be resolved. The peace (shalom) of God will not come in its fullness until then.

What is the Bible's hope and promise for creation? Both Testaments teach that the Redeemer God has His entire creation in sight as the object of final redemption. God's kingdom includes full reconciliation between nature and humanity and overcoming the tragic interplay between the two. This is an essential part of the Christian hope.

According to Isaiah, creation was not just an event of the past. In the new age that Isaiah heralds, God will make all things new. In the new creation no boundary will exist between 'nature' and 'history', because both human life and the natural order will be marvellously transformed.[4] Even the wilderness will be converted into a garden like Eden (Isa. 41:18–20; 51:3).

Listen to Paul's breathtaking understanding of God's plans for the natural order:

> The creation waits with eager longing for the revealing of the children of God; for the creation was subjected to futility, not of its own will but by the will of the one who subjected it, in hope that the creation itself will be set free from its bondage to decay and will obtain the freedom of the glory of the children of God. We know that the whole creation has been groaning in labor pains until now; and not only the creation, but we ourselves, who have the first fruits of the Spirit, groan inwardly while we wait for adoption, the redemption of our bodies. (Rom. 8:19–23, NRSV)

Paul's expectation is consistent with what he as a Jew believed regarding creation and the Redeemer God. It would have been inconceivable to him that God would devise a plan of redemption that would leave out part of His creation. God doesn't abandon what He creates. God could not do so without calling into question His own faithfulness. Paul's vision of God's relationship to creation helps us understand what he says about the resurrection (1 Cor. 15:35–57).

Just as the Bible begins by saying good things about creation's origin, it closes by telling us that some day God will renew creation (Rev. 21:1–8). John folds Isaiah's promise of creation's renewal into what Christians can expect when Jesus completes the kingdom of His Father (Isa. 65:17; 66:22). The whole story of God urges us not to despair over the tragic qualities of nature and humanity's collision with it.

If God were to wash His hands of creation, we would have reason to despair. Tragedy would then issue the final word. Admittedly, human suffering resulting from tragic encounters with nature often tempts us to despair. But because of God's nearness to creation, neither tragedy nor despair will ever have the final say.

Just how close is God to His creation? Again, let Paul answer: 'He [Christ] is the image of the invisible God, the firstborn over all creation. For by him all things were created: things in heaven and on earth, visible and invisible ... all things were created by him and for him. He is before all things, and in him all things hold together' (Col. 1:15–17).

This Christ who is the 'glue' and 'goal' of the universe will ensure that what Paul anticipates in Romans 8:19–23 will indeed occur.

Patiently, *creation waits in faith and hope. It waits with eager longing* for the revealing of God's children (Rom. 8:19). Those words provide the key to understanding how Christians should pray and express faith in the presence of tragedy.

First, we must do so in total honesty. Without resorting to easy solutions, we realise tragedy is real in human life.

Second, we deal with tragedy by letting God's grace redeem it in all possible circumstances.

Third, where tragedy cannot now be overcome, we believe Christ's peace reaches into its depths.

Finally, the good news about Christ's resurrection, our 'eager longing' and hope, teaches us that tragedy, though baffling and oppressive, will not speak the last word for God's people and creation. Both the creation and we 'will be liberated from its bondage' (Rom. 8:21).

06

If Christ is victor, why does evil still run loose in the world?

THE MYSTERY OF INIQUITY

We come now to what many Christians think is their most persistent obstacle to prayer: the reality of unrelenting evil in a world where God has supposedly placed all things in heaven and earth under the reign of His risen Son.

The New Testament claims that all powers, visible or invisible, are made to serve the ascended Lord. But many Christians continue to confront evil in their own and others' lives. They observe how sin and the powers of darkness pour destruction into the lives of persons, families and nations. And they are deeply troubled by the apparent contradiction between the New Testament claims and what they experience and observe.

While many Christians seem able to skip over the apparent conflict between the presence of evil and the claims in the New Testament about Christ, many cannot. Their inability either to live with or to resolve the apparent contradiction obstructs prayer. They simply don't know how to pray confidently and intelligently. Sometimes they pray that evil will be put to flight in their own families, and it seems that Christ answers prayer. He scatters the powers of evil and demonstrates that He is Lord.

In other equally desperate instances when Christians cry out to the reigning Lord, nothing seems to happen. Evil continues to thrive. Spouse abuse continues. A son commits suicide anyway. Has Jesus really disarmed the powers and principalities? Then what are we to make of the following story from the 28 July, 2001 edition of the *New York Times*? Today a European sex slave industry thrives and is centred in Velesta, Macedonia. Across the Balkans, tens of thousands of women have been at least temporarily enslaved by sex traffickers. The women have suffered rape, extreme violence and slavery at the hands of criminal groups famous for their brutality and greed. A network of traffickers moves the women across borders and ethnic communities. The network spreads across the Balkans and into Western Europe. A decade of conflict in the region and the grinding poverty of post-Communist Eastern Europe have helped breed the network.[1]

What about the lies and gossip that terminate people's ministries? And let's not forget the infidelity that ends marriages, the violent assaults that end lives, and the bribes and greed that corrupt nations. For many Christians, rather than praying to the One who rules over the powers, it seems more like playing a random cosmic lottery. In prayer, we just have to take our chances. It sometimes seems that on the matter of evil and who is ahead in the struggle, the jury is still out.

Such language may seem abrasive to some Christians. To others it is honest. God's sovereignty seems to be in question.

We can choose to avoid raising such questions. We can

maintain comfort and aloof stability. But comfort and stability will come at a terrible price. Our comfort will leave behind many sincere Christians whose prayers, faith, and action have nearly been immobilised by the tenacity of moral evil.

Do we want to admit that the New Testament's marvellous claims about Jesus can survive only in an incubator? Must Jesus be sheltered against the often-harsh elements of life?

Of course not. But this means we can't skirt the questions that anguished Christians raise to God.

'Chomp' or 'lights in the trees'?

As Annie Dillard spent her year at Tinker Creek observing the natural world, she repeatedly encountered a question: What is nature's truth? Are beauty, design and purpose nature's truth? Or does its truth finally turn out to be 'chomp, crunch'?

Does the world lead us to conclude that a wise and purposeful Creator authored it? Or is mindless, purposeless waste what the world finally forces us to admit? The evidence Dillard offers so powerfully in *Pilgrim at Tinker Creek* seems hopelessly mixed.

Let's say you're a female ichneumon fly (a wasp-like insect with worm-like larvae that are parasites in or on other insects). You have mated and your eggs are fertile. Your young will starve if you can't find a caterpillar on which to lay your eggs. You know that when the eggs hatch, the young will eat anybody on which they find themselves – including you. So if you can't find a caterpillar, you must broadcast the eggs over the fields, but then the eggs will hatch and your young will starve – and you will have died of old age before then. 'You feel them coming, and coming, and you struggle to rise.'[2]

Or what about the female lacewing? Lacewings are

fragile green insects with large, rounded transparent wings. Sometimes when a female lacewing lays her fertile eggs on a green leaf, she becomes hungry. She stops laying eggs momentarily, turns around, and one by one eats the eggs she has just laid. Then she lays some more and eats them too.[3]

But Dillard has also seen nature's beauty. She has been struck by its unfathomable intricacy.[4] 'Do you know,' she asks, 'that in the head of the caterpillar of the ordinary goat moth there are two hundred twenty-eight muscles?'[5] She sees evidence that nature is not a roughed-in sketch, but that it is 'supremely, meticulously, created, created abundantly, extravagantly'.[6]

When surgeons learned how to remove cataracts, they went across Europe and America operating on people who had since birth been blinded by cataracts. Many doctors tested their patients' sense of perceptions and ideas of space both before and after the operations.

When the surgeon removed the bandages from the eyes of a little girl whom they had operated on, they took the child into a garden. She was astonished by what she saw and stood speechless in front of a tree. As she gazed into the tree, with sunlight streaming through it, she exclaimed, 'The tree has lights in it.'[7]

Annie tells us that through a peach orchard in summer and in the forests in the autumn, she had searched for 'the tree with the lights in it'. Then one day she was walking along Tinker Creek,

> ... and I saw the tree with the lights in it. I saw the backyard cedar where the mourning doves roost charged and transfigured, each cell buzzing with flame. I stood on the grass with the lights in it, grass that was

wholly fire, utterly focused and utterly dreamed. It was less like seeing than like being for the first time seen, knocked breathless by a powerful glance. The flood of fire abated, but I am still spending the power.[8]

Because of what she saw, her right foot now says, 'Amen!' and her left foot says, 'Hallelujah!'[9]

Nature cannot answer the question it raises. The evidence is inconclusive. Is the beauty that Dillard has seen actually 'an intricately fashioned lure, the cruelest hoax of all'?[10] She finally admits that much of what she has seen at Tinker Creek 'buoys her up'. But much of what she has seen 'drags her down'.[11] Annie wonders if the designed intricacy she thinks she sees is not after all 'inaccurate and lopsided?'[12] Taking either path can 'lead to madness'.[13]

Like many Christians, Dillard is perplexed over the conflict between what she believes about a God who created and governs the world and the evil – both moral and natural – she sees in the world. If she were to deny this conflict she would go mad.

The Hebrews, Dillard thinks, must have shared her struggles. She describes two offerings the Hebrews made to God. One was the 'wave offering' and the other was the 'heave offering'. She says the 'wave offering' was an offering of thanksgiving. The Hebrews worshipped God for His orderly governance of the world, for His mercy, and for His steadfast faithfulness. But the 'heave offering' was something else. Whereas the wave offering was waved before the Lord, the heave offering was heaved or thrown. Dillard wants to know, 'Did the priest hurl the shoulder of the ram of consecration across the tabernacle *at* God?'

The ram of consecration had been perfect and whole,

not 'blind, or broken, or maimed, or having a [benign skin tumour], or scurvy, or scabbed ... bruised, or crushed, or broken, or cut'.[14] Did the priest, by heaving the shoulder at God mean to say for himself and all of Israel, 'Look what you made me do ... God, *look* at the sorrow, the cruelty, the long ... waste!'[15] Did the two offerings show the Hebrews' awareness of the world's mixed signals and of evil's presence when it should not be there?

Like many of God's people, Annie Dillard pondered her questions. 'We are people,' she says. 'We are permitted to have dealings with the Creator', and we must ask these questions.

If we move a short distance from Tinker Creek we'll meet innocent children who have been brutalised by drug-ridden parents. We'll find little girls in southern Sudan who have been forced into sexual slavery. Closer to home are infants born with heroin addiction and alcohol syndrome. All of this, mind you, in a world where Christians say the kingdom of God has been inaugurated. Aren't Christians the ones who say that when the kingdom of God came in Jesus of Nazareth, the world changed fundamentally? Isn't that what the Old Testament promised regarding the kingdom of God?

Keo Chantha, 23, is at the centre of a new and accelerating crisis confronting Cambodia. Just as the country is emerging from three decades of civil war and mass killings, it is facing a new scourge: AIDS. Cambodia is the sickest country in Asia; gaunt figures dot the cities and scattered villages. The people look like the starving victims of the Khmer Rouge years.

Keo Chantha has AIDS. She is bald and spends her days scratching her scabs. Except for her radiant smile, nothing is left of her former beauty. She and 12 other patients wait out their days at the Maryknoll hospice, shivering and coughing under their blankets.

Keo Chantha is a prostitute. That's how she contracted AIDS. No one knows how many men she has infected. They would be men like Touch Saroeun, a weak and wasted man of 31 with large, glowing eyes and the stunned look of someone who has been ambushed.

Hold on! Before we say, 'Well, Keo, you had it coming,' hear the rest of her story: when Keo was 14, her brother sold her into prostitution.[16]

CHRIST THE VICTOR?

The New Testament claims that the resurrected Christ now reigns in the Church and in the world. We are told He is Lord of all and that our prayers are offered to this One who sits at the Father's right hand. He now reigns over the powers and principalities. They have become subject to Him. Listen to what the New Testament says God has accomplished in His Son. God 'disarmed the powers and authorities, he made a public spectacle of them, triumphing over them by the cross' (Col. 2:15). This means that as the crucified, resurrected and ascended Lord, Christ has taken all evil powers captive. He has stripped them of their armour. Their humiliation in the world is a grand display of our Lord's victory.

Let's hear more about what the New Testament claims. When exhorting the Christians in Ephesus to live in the unity of the Spirit, Paul said that God is the Father of all. He is 'over all and through all and in all' (Eph. 4:6). Through His death, descent into 'the lower earthly regions', resurrection, and ascension, Christ has taken captive all spiritual powers hostile to God (Eph. 4:1–10). How extensive is Christ's domination of the powers of evil He has conquered? God has put His immeasurable power to work in Christ when He raised Him from the dead and seated Him at His right hand in the heavenly places.

God has placed His ascended Son 'far above all rule and authority, and power and dominion, and every title that can be given, not only in the present age but also in the one to come. And God placed all things under his feet and appointed him to be head over everything for the church, which is his body, the fulness of him who fills everything in every way' (Eph. 1:21–23; see also 1 Cor. 15:27).

Our Lord is Christ the Victor. Every power in all creation that would stand against Him has been forced into submission and servitude. He has publicly humiliated them (Col. 2:15). Through Christ all things were created, things in heaven and on earth. He created both visible and invisible powers as well as thrones, dominions and principalities. All things were 'created by him and for him' (Col. 1:16). The rebellious powers that once rampaged throughout God's creation are now subject to Christ, who reigns at the Father's right hand.

But if this is true, many Christians want to know, why does evil still molest the world that Christ supposedly rules? If Christ is victor, why do looters rush in after a hurricane? Why do mothers intentionally abort unborn children? If Christ is victor, why do the powers actually assume kingdom-like qualities? Think, for example, of the kingdom of drug trafficking that wastes minds, families and even whole nations. Recall the kingdom of racial hatred and the kingdom of sexual exploitation. Remember the kingdom of economic exploitation that permits tobacco companies, for example, with government protection, to offload their oversupply of cigarettes in Third-World countries.

What should we make of the kingdoms of evil that protect child pornography and kidnap children to be sold into sexual slavery? Can anyone forget the kingdom of evil that entices and deceives young women in Thailand and Vietnam into an industry that promotes sex tours organised by promoters in the United States, Canada and Europe? If in the cross and resurrection, the powers of evil were submitted to Christ, why are governments so easily corrupted? Why must children in poorer communities receive substandard education? Are the 'powers' really under Christ's control?

THE GRACE THAT 'SEES' DIFFERENTLY

So what are Christians to do amid militant and undeniable evil? How shall we respond to the fact that not all things have in fact been put under His feet? Should we just put our faith on hold? Should we declare a break in our determination to embrace and follow the resurrected Christ? Should we just tell the Lord that when we see much better evidence in His favour, then we'll put our full, unwavering faith in Him? Maybe at that point prayer would not be so ambiguous and conflicted.

That depends on what you have 'seen', says Annie Dillard. There is, she says, a certain kind of 'seeing' that involves a 'letting go'.[17] The secret of 'seeing', she says, 'is the pearl of great price'.[18] But, Annie, after having seen evil in the world, and after admitting how evil seems to contradict what the New Testament says about Christ taking the powers captive, what is left to 'see'?

Hendrik Berkhof answers this question and would agree with Dillard. It all depends on what one 'sees'.

First, Berkhof says, a Christian must 'see' that in the crucifixion of Jesus, the powers of evil and their enmity towards God were fully manifest. They have been un-masked, their 'cover' blown. Now we clearly know who they are. Berkhof says the evil powers are not only overt and destructive evil, but they are also the evil that parades as a love for God's Law and that can even appear in His Church.

In fact, representatives of these powers called for Jesus' crucifixion in the name of the Law. Jesus condemned these powers and their representatives for loving darkness rather than light (John 3:19). The priests wanted Jesus crucified in the name of the Temple. The Pharisees called for Jesus' crucifixion in the name of piety. The crucifixion showed what Roman justice is worth when called upon to serve the Truth Himself.[19]

Never again can the powers of evil successfully parade as anything except God's enemies. In the cross they have been exposed to the truth and to public humiliation. 'See – this is what you are, and Jesus is your limit.'

Second, not only has evil been fully exposed for what it is, but on the cross Christ put an *end* to the workings of evil. If after having played their strongest hand, if after implementing their most dastardly scheme, the powers of evil were to be unsuccessful, then their *end* would have come. This would be true no matter how much noise they might make in the throes of death. This is exactly what happened.

In fact, and in anticipation, in the cross God put an *end* to the powers of evil. In faithful obedience, Jesus took upon Himself the sin of the world. He absorbed the worst blow hell could deliver against the holy and loving God. But He did not fold and did not flee. He did not reverse His being on the cross, even though some who looked on baited Him to do so (Luke 23:35). On the cross the Son of God engaged all the powers of hell that could possibly molest the Church. He struggled against sin's hold upon creation and humanity. He nailed to the cross the guilt before God that was rightfully ours (Col. 2:13–15).

Christ also put an *end* to the powers by anticipating Easter. What if, after the powers of evil have delivered their strongest punch, have committed and expended all of their forces, Jesus didn't 'stay dead'? What if on Easter morning the God who created the heavens and the earth were to raise His Son to new life? What if Jesus is now alive forevermore, being both the Alpha and the Omega?

This is what Annie Dillard and Berkhof have in mind when they invite us to 'see'. This is what the children of God must clearly see if they are to avoid the veto on hope that evil wants to impose on God, His Church and His world. Unless a person sees this, he or she will limp along in the shadows of the gospel, never to leap in its glory. They will never be able to step as Annie Dillard did, with the right foot singing, 'Hallelujah!' and the left foot shouting, 'Amen!'

Annie Dillard doesn't try to avoid the fact that she sees evil in the world. But she also knows she has received grace. And grace is the most important reality of all. This is the grace that overcomes evil at its worst. Therefore, because she has received grace, and knows this without question, she refuses to 'sulk along the rest of her days on the edge of rage'. If Christians understand that they have received grace, if they have 'seen the light in the tree', or better yet, the light on the tree, then they should be making 'whoopee' instead of making 'hay'. Christians should be 'raising Lazarus' instead of raising 'tomatoes'.[20]

Christians are people who 'see' because they are the 'children of light' (John 12:36). They 'see' that Christ has put an *end* to the powers of evil. The cross and resurrection of Christ are their 'light in the trees'. Christ has unmasked and disarmed the powers. But this doesn't mean that with one blow their ungodly working has ceased.

Swiss theologian Karl Barth put it this way: 'The battle has been won decisively; now the mopping-up campaign needs to be completed.'

Hendrik Berkhof puts it somewhat differently: 'In principle the victory is certain; yet the battle continues until the triumph will have become effective on all fronts and visible to all.'[21] He tells of the 1944–45 'hunger winter' in the Netherlands through which he lived. The Allies had defeated the Nazis, but the remaining Nazis whose fate had been sealed were still oppressing the Dutch.[22]

Listen to Paul's words that speak of the 'not yet' side of the 'already'. 'For our struggle is not against flesh and blood, but against the rulers, against the authorities, against the powers of this dark world and against the spiritual forces of evil in the heavenly realms' (Eph. 6:12). From bitter experience, the apostle knew the 'ruler of the kingdom of the air' is the spirit 'now at work in those who are disobedient' (Eph. 2:2). He knew that through the resurrected and reigning Christ the manifold wisdom of God is still being made known 'to the rulers and authorities in the heavenly realms' (Eph. 3:10). Nevertheless, this same Christ has *already* 'disarmed the powers and authorities', and 'made a public spectacle of them, triumphing over them by the cross' (Col. 2:15).

Even now, children of the kingdom walk, not according to the flesh and the powers of evil, but according to the Holy Spirit. The Spirit of God dwells in them. This is the Spirit of the Father who unmasked and humiliated the powers of evil when He raised Jesus from the dead. Christians know God has broken the power and hold of sin in them. As new creatures, now the Father who raised Jesus from the dead gives life to our mortal bodies through the Holy Spirit who dwells in us. Those in whom the Spirit dwells will set their minds on things of the Spirit. Doing so is life and peace (Rom. 8:1–11). This is the quality of Christian life Christ has won for all His brothers and sisters. There are no elites here. There is no quota of 'haves' and 'have nots'.

Some of Jesus' sisters and brothers still await the full measure of that inner peace and certainty. Jesus holds and carries them. He is their patient Mediator before the Father.

For those who by the Holy Spirit 'see', the distinction between the 'already' and the 'not yet' is not a contradiction. The evil generated by the powers of darkness displays acts of frenzied desperation, not acts of victory. Broken and desperate, the powers resort to oppression and persecution. But, as Berkhof points out, in their desperation 'their unmasking is repeated and confirmed. They can no longer exist without being forced to uncover their true nature and thereby to abandon their role as gods and saviors.'[23]

We Christians who speak, act or pray as though the outcome of the battle is still in question, need again to be led by Jesus to the cross and the empty tomb. In fact, in the face of the horrible evils that ravage lives and nations, all of us must have many of those reassuring and restorative moments. Through prayer, Bible reading, proclaiming of the gospel, the sacraments and in Christian community, Jesus will repeatedly invite us, 'Put your finger here; see my hands. Reach out your hand and put it into my side. Stop doubting and believe.' In the presence of numbing evil, the Spirit of God will renew in us the confession, 'My Lord and my God!' (John 20:27–28).

So how may Christians pray confidently and intelligently

in a world where 'the mystery of iniquity' (2 Thess. 2:7, KJV) still works? Should we just ignore the work of the rulers of darkness? Should we act as though it's nothing? Should we just find ways to fit every abused child and every raped woman into God's plan to bring about good? Or maybe we should recognise evil for what it is and then isolate ourselves from the sufferings that reveal the desperate activity of the powers of evil. Nonsense!

The cross of Christ commissions us to recognise evil for exactly what it is: an all-out effort to kill God. In the power of the Spirit we must confront it and struggle against it in all its forms. Otherwise, we will break faith with the power of the cross and resurrection, with suffering humanity and with suffering creation.

Christians should not hide. We should never minimise the works of hell that stalk our youth, families, governments and nations. Never! In the power and meaning of the resurrection of our Lord, we confront the powers of evil head-on.

Fully facing the 'powers and principalities' now desperately working on a thousand fronts, Christians are to pray in the power and confidence of the cross and resurrection of our Lord. We must be wary of the danger of seeing only the mixed evidence of 'chomp' and 'lights' this world offers. Christians are to pray as people who see that the kingdoms of this world are becoming the kingdoms of our Lord.

Further, Christians must pray as people who suffer with a suffering world. Here the meaning of intercessory prayer rises to its zenith. Such an invitation will not be received by that brand of popular Christianity that crafts discipleship without suffering, a gospel without a cross, and a God without judgment. That, Dietrich Bonhoeffer said, is the 'cheap grace' sold in the marketplace like cheap wares.

Costly grace, Jesus told us, demands that we take up our cross daily and follow Him (Luke 9:23). The apostle Peter said Christians are called to participate in Christ's sufferings (1 Pet. 4:13). One way Christians can do this is to suffer with a suffering world, and one way we can achieve this is through intercessory prayer.

We can also suffer by pursuing justice and by acting mercifully. To do so, we must put on the whole armour of God. Only then can we hope to stand against the wiles of the devil. For our struggle is 'against the rulers, against the authorities, against the powers of this dark world and against the spiritual forces of evil in the heavenly realms' (Eph. 6:12).

The writer to the Hebrews says that God has subjected all things to Jesus. God left nothing out of His control. Then almost as if to contradict himself, the writer says, 'Yet at present we do not see everything subject to him.'

So which one is it? The answer is that on the basis of what we have already 'seen' and 'known', we are certain the deed is done. What has yet to be 'subjected' is just a matter of extending the lines of the 'already'. 'But we see Jesus ... now crowned with glory and honour because he suffered death ...' (Heb. 2:9).

Who, Karl Barth asked, is this Jesus to whom Christians pray? Who is this One who shows the presence of the mystery of iniquity, who is this One in whom they place their trust?

Barth answers that He is God's act of salvation. He is the Word of God. He declares and shows that the cosmos, people and each individual are not alone. Even though Satan roars like a lion, God the Creator has not abandoned His creation. Because of Jesus, we are not left to our own defences. He, and not the yawning canyon of evil, will have the final word.[24]

Did we in our own strength confide,
    Our striving would be losing;
Were not the right Man on our side,
    The Man of God's own choosing.
Dost ask who that may be?
Christ Jesus – it is He;
Lord Sabaoth, His name,
From age to age the same;
And He must win the battle.
And tho' this world, with devils filled,
    Should threaten to undo us,
We will not fear, for God hath willed
    His truth to triumph through us.
The prince of darkness grim –
We tremble not for him.
His rage we can endure,
For, lo, his doom is sure;
One little word shall fell him.

                    –Martin Luther

07

The God who holds us

On Thursday, 16 March, 2001, Kenneth Waters, 47 years old, saw a mobile phone for the first time, drank his first Starbucks coffee and ate his first corned-beef sandwich in two decades. Waters had just emerged from 18 years in prison for a crime he did not commit. His murder conviction had been overturned by newly tested DNA evidence.

As Waters emerged from a courtroom in Cambridge, Massachusetts, exuberant family members, including some he had never met, hugged him.

'It's great to be free,' he said.

One relative who greeted Kenneth was his sister, Betty Anne Waters. When in 1980 Kenneth was convicted of murdering Katharina Brow, Betty Anne refused to accept the verdict. Nor did his family lose faith in Kenneth's innocence. Betty Anne's confidence in her brother's innocence changed her life.

She was still a young mother of two children when Kenneth was convicted. She had dropped out of high school. But she was so determined to exonerate her brother that she completed high school and went to college. Next, she was accepted into law school and worked her way through until she eventually became her brother's attorney. Betty Anne waged an extraordinary legal battle that led to Kenneth's release.

'There was no alternative,' Betty Anne joked. 'We were out of money for lawyers.' She began writing to the New York-based Innocence Project and hunted down the old blood samples in her brother's case. With the help of another attorney and the Innocence Project, in 1999 Betty Anne asked for her brother's DNA to be tested against the old blood samples. The results came in: they did not match. Betty Anne and attorney Barry Scheck filed a motion for a new trial. Prosecutors agreed that overturning the conviction 'would be in the interest of justice'.

Betty Anne's commitment to proving her brother's innocence is astonishing. By the time she walked out of the courthouse on 16 March 2001, hand-in-hand with her brother, she had spent 18 years in unbroken service to him. What a covenant! As she left the courthouse, she said, 'I don't think I've had a better day.'[1]

Betty Anne Waters' steadfast refusal to abandon her brother provides a beautiful window into understanding the meaning and character of Christian hope. The story can also serve as a parable of God's unfailing love.

Christian hope is a central theme in the New Testament. The gospel and hope are inseparable. In fact, the apostle Paul calls God 'the God of hope' (Rom. 15:13). The Christian gospel is the gospel of hope.

In this chapter we explore some of the rich dimensions of Christian hope, particularly as they relate to prayer. Many are the Christians for whom crises, failures, sufferings, depression, abandonment by others and persecution, have drained their awareness of hope. Quiet despair or even resentment against

God is more their companion. Some actually feel as though God has abandoned them.

When a sense of hopelessness afflicts Christians, they may find it nearly impossible to pray. An inability to pray usually feeds the sense of hopelessness. Defeat thickens. Frustration replaces hope. The world and God seem to shut down.

A friend of mine is a noted brain researcher. We have had many delightful conversations regarding the relationship between Christian faith and how the brain works. Once we were discussing brain chemistry. He was explaining the importance of Seratonin, a neurotransmitter involved in human mood disorders. He told me that by lowering Seratonin, one could eliminate a person's sense of hope. Another friend watches closely for government approval in the States of new drugs that will more effectively create a longer use of the neurotransmitters and hence offset the effect of lowered Seratonin. The second friend says, 'People like me live for the magic bullet that will put us out of our daily pain.'

It's not surprising that brain chemistry can negatively affect our sense of hope. But my friend the brain researcher was both correct and incorrect. Having *a sense* or *feeling of hope* is one thing; being *in Christian hope* is quite another. We need to more carefully examine the nature of Christian hope.

Let's return to Betty Anne Waters and her brother Kenneth. Who held whom in the story? There must have been times in prison when Kenneth flirted with the idea of giving up. Often he must have fought despair. Can you imagine sitting in prison for 18 years, knowing you didn't commit the crime for which you were sentenced? Can you comprehend the loneliness and pointlessness of it all? There must have been times when Kenneth fought hard to 'hold on'.

But the key to Kenneth's release from prison wasn't *what* he held onto. The key was *who* held on to him. In this remarkable story of love for a brother, Mary Anne held onto Kenneth even when hopelessness threatened to overtake him. Clearly, Kenneth's holding on was of secondary importance. Betty Anne's commitment to her brother was of primary importance. Had Betty Anne been less committed to his release than Kenneth himself, he would probably still be in jail.

We often speak of Christians as 'having hope'. In a secondary sense this is true, and our active participation should not be overlooked. But we're not the primary authors of hope. If we were, then all of us would be in fatal trouble. Instead, *God* is the author of hope. He gives hope to us. In the New Testament, Christian hope is not first of all about what *we* hold, but about *who* holds *us*. It has nothing to do with whether of nor we can 'feel' hope. We may feel absolutely hopeless and still be firmly grounded in hope.

Christian hope arises from and is secured by the resurrection of Jesus Christ. In raising Jesus from the grave, the Father gave unmistakable confirmation that His Son had faithfully borne witness to His Father. Jesus came proclaiming the coming of the kingdom of God (Mark 1:14–15). God's long-anticipated reign in all the earth and over all nations had begun. A new order had been inaugurated. Sinners and the poor could gladly receive the gospel of the kingdom. No one before had ever told them that even they could become the children of God. No one had said that they could address God as their Abba (Father).

'The Spirit of the Lord is on me,' Jesus proclaimed, 'because he has anointed me to preach good news to the poor. He has sent me to proclaim freedom for the prisoners and recovery of sight for the blind, to release the oppressed, to proclaim the year of the Lord's favour' (Luke 4:18–19). The four Gospels record instance after instance of how gladly sinners, captives, and the poor received Jesus. Sometimes sinners pushed in so closely to hear Jesus that the religious leaders became angry (Luke 15:1–2).

Then on Easter morning, the Father proclaimed, 'All that My Son has said about Me is true. He is My Amen.' The apostle Paul summarises the matter in this way: 'For no matter how many promises God has made, they are "Yes" in Christ. And so through him the "Amen" is spoken by us to the glory of God' (2 Cor. 1:20).

Christian hope is the gift that God's 'Amen' gives to us. It is the confidence that God's 'Amen' will complete the kingdom that He inaugurated. Because we already know Jesus, God's 'Amen', we already know the future. And we who are Jesus' sisters and brothers are included. Through the Spirit we say, 'Amen', to God's 'Amen'. Having Christian hope means being received into the future of our resurrected Lord (1 Cor. 15:12–28).

To understand all this, let's compare a mother monkey and a mother cat. When a mother monkey wants to move her babies, they must hold on to her for dear life. The journey depends largely on the babies. But when a mother cat wants to move her kittens, she uses her teeth to take each one by the nape of the neck and carry it to the new resting place. The kitten may not 'feel' like going, but it's off to new quarters anyway.

Christian hope is the Church's glad confidence that the God who has so magnificently shown His salvation in Christ will complete all He began to do. It is the joyous anticipation that He who *has* come *will* come again (1 Pet. 1:3–5) and that the kingdoms of this world *are* becoming the kingdoms of our Lord (Rev. 11:15).

Christian hope is the highest conceivable form of certainty.

When the word 'hope' enters the Christian arena, it no longer means what it does on a purely human level. For us to say, 'I hope we have enough petrol to make it home', does not have the same content as saying, 'My hope is in the resurrection of our Lord.' The first hope rests on uncertainty, the second on certainty. Paul speaks of Christian hope by saying, how great is 'the glory of that which lasts'. He says that we should therefore be 'very bold' (2 Cor. 3:11–12).

Christian hope results from the faithful God giving Himself to us, filling and lifting us through the power of the Holy Spirit. From the human side, hope is the Church's worshipful and obedient confidence in its Lord. Paul assured us that this hope will keep us from being disappointed (Rom. 5:5).

Even under persecution, can Christians actively rejoice in the reality of Christian hope (Rom. 5:2)? Hear how Paul prayed for the Roman Christians: 'May the God of hope fill you with all joy and peace as you trust in him, so that you may overflow with hope by the power of the Holy Spirit' (15:13).

To be a full recipient of Christian hope, must we *feel* this is true? No! One may be a child of hope and at times still feel hopeless, abandoned, defeated, depressed and faithless. Even then hope carries us. Can we be held securely by Christian hope even when we can't pray? Yes, indeed!

Thomas Merton (1915–68), American writer and Trappist monk, voiced this confidence:

MY LORD GOD, I have no idea where I am going I do not see the road ahead of me. I cannot know for certain where it will all end. Nor do I really know myself, and the fact that I think that I am following your will does not mean that I am actually doing so. But I believe that the desire to please you does in fact please you. And

I hope I have that desire in all I am doing. I hope that
I will never do anything apart from that desire. And I
know that if I do this you will lead me by the right road
though I may know nothing about it. Therefore will I
trust you always though I may seem to be lost and in the
shadow of death. I will not fear, for you are ever with me,
and you will never leave me to face my perils alone.[2]

How should our knowledge of how God holds us affect
our prayers? We begin by asking the Lord to clear away our
misconceptions regarding Christian hope. This may take
some time. Then, as simply and in as elementary a form as is
necessary, we begin to place our trust in the God who holds
us, the God of hope. The Holy Spirit will help us. Our first
steps may be uncertain and lack a sense of hope. Never mind.
We have laid to rest the misperception that turns discipleship
into a performance-based enterprise.

In Christian hope God holds us in a certainty born of
Easter, nourished by the Holy Spirit and cultivated in the
life of the Church of Christ. No wonder Revelation, written
during persecution in the Church, nevertheless proclaims,

'See, the home of God is among mortals.
He will dwell with them as their God;
they will be his peoples,
and God himself will be with them;
he will wipe every tear from their eyes.
Death will be no more;
mourning and crying and pain will be no more,
for the first things have passed away.'
And the one who was seated on the throne said,
'See, I am making all things new.' (21:3–5, NRSV)

The Bible tells the story of the God who gives Himself to us. He did this long before we knew He had. The Old Testament says that when Israel was young, God carried it as a father carries a child. In the New Testament this is true of how Christ carries His sisters and brothers. Christ has a word of promise when we're tempted to think that because of despair, depression, failure or illness we are strangers to hope. Our prayers may even fall back on us like a suffocating weight. Jesus says, "Do not be afraid. I am the First and the Last. I am the Living One; I was dead, and behold I am alive for ever and ever! And I hold the keys of death and Hades' (Rev. 1:17–18). Amen.

08

Texts of frustration

F.B. Meyer (1847–1929), the well-known baptist minister who introduced D.L. Moody to churches in England, penned an insightful tribute to the Scriptures. The Bible is, he said, the storehouse of the promises of God. 'It is the sword of the Spirit, before which temptation flees. It is the all-sufficient equipment of Christian usefulness. It is the believer's guidebook and directory in all possible circumstances.'[1]

Of all the aids to prayer through the ages, none compares in importance to the Holy Scriptures. No one can hope to become a friend of God who does not become a friend of God's Word, the inspired and authoritative witness to Him.

George Müller (1805–98), who started orphanages in England that provided for the spiritual, educational and physical needs of over 2,000 boys and girls, said,

> It often astonishes me that I did not see the importance of meditation upon the Scripture earlier in my Christian life ... What is the food for the inner man? Not prayer, but the Word of God – not the simple reading of the

Word of God, so that it only passes through our minds ...
No, we must consider what we read, ponder over it, and
apply it to our hearts.[2]

The Bible faithfully tells God's story and our story as
His people. When enlivened by the Holy Spirit, the Bible
faithfully bears witness to Christ, who is the incarnate Word
of God. He is the One to whom the Scriptures point and to
whom they lead us. No one can hope to pray effectively who
fails to be tutored by the Scriptures.

Karl Barth said that when the witness of the New
Testament encounters us, we must give up trying to be in
control. We can no longer be neutral. The New Testament,
Barth said, grasps us and tells us 'what we have to let
ourselves be told: who and what is real and true, Jesus Christ
as Lord, and we as His'.

The New Testament grasps us not principally to impart
information but to place God's claim on us. It lays hold of us
and issues a demand that we receive its message and become
witnesses to the living God. When the New Testament takes
hold of us, Barth said, it binds us to wrestle with the gospel.
In its presence we must end all 'pretexts and caprices'.[3]

But as inspiring as Meyer's and Barth's words may be, we
must also recognise that parts of the New Testament – especially
some of Jesus' words dealing with prayer – generate serious
problems for some Christians. For them, parts of the New
Testament are the problem. If we want to be faithful to those
who 'cannot pray', we must pay attention to their reasons.

For many Christians, rather than calling us to 'wrestle
with the gospel' as Barth said, negative experiences with
prayer in response to the New Testament, have turned some
texts into sources of failure. For them, parts of the New

Testament have become 'texts of frustration'.

Let's examine some of the better-known 'texts of frustration'. Hopefully we can remove the frustrations and bring the verses to life again. Maybe with the Spirit's assistance, the texts of frustration can again clearly convey the part of the gospel they were meant to communicate. Perhaps the texts will again, as Barth hoped, 'lay hold of us' and make us lively 'witnesses' to their message. Hopefully they will become 'texts of encouragement' for honest hearts that sincerely want to pray effectively and trust God completely.

The texts of frustration are found in Matthew 7:7–8; 18:18–19; 21:22; Luke 11:5–13; 18:1, 6; and John 16:23–24.

I have consulted a series of respected Bible commentaries and will not here, for purposes of readability, identify the sources for each textual explanation.[4]

THE MATTHEW TEXTS

1. Matthew 7:7–8 (paralleled in Luke 11:9–10). 'Ask, and it will be given you; search, and you will find; knock, and the door will be opened for you. For everyone who asks receives, and everyone who searches finds, and for everyone who knocks, the door will be opened' (NRSV).

'Ask, and it will be given you.' 'Everyone who asks receives.' This is part of Jesus' Sermon on the Mount (5:1–7:27). The three imperatives (commands), 'Ask', 'search', and 'knock' express a confident attitude towards the heavenly Father. No conditions are attached to them. Jesus does not tell us what to request, what to search for or what we are to find. The object seems to be the 'good things' of verse 11.

The three promises – 'receive', 'find', 'open' – seem unqualified. Regarding prayer, do the unqualified statements guarantee what they appear to promise? Is it really true that whatever we ask for in the name of Jesus we will receive? If we seek, will we find without limitations?

If so, what should we tell Cynthia, who desperately prayed that her alcoholic husband would be saved? She asked, she sought and she knocked on heaven's door until the day her husband died in a horrible head-on collision while having a blood alcohol level that went through the ceiling. She had read and believed Matthew 7:7–8. But the promises did not materialise. For her these verses have become a text of frustration.

Explanation. Some scholars think these verses should be connected to the preceding ones in which Jesus warns against judging people who have 'specks' in their eyes. The judges have 'logs' in their own eyes. These scholars say that verses 7 and 8 teach that rather than trying to remove the specks ourselves, we should ask God to remove them.

Having warned His disciples against judging others, Jesus exhorts them to pray. He assures them that if they pray in this way, their prayer for the neighbour will be heard. So according to these scholars, Matthew 7:7–8 has nothing to do with unqualified promises to those who make requests to God.

But other equally competent scholars say there's no connection between Matthew 7:7–8 and the preceding verses. They say that verses 7 to 11 form a self-contained unit. Others say that in these verses Jesus makes promises to the disciples for their work in proclaiming the kingdom of God. God will supply their needs as they announce the gospel. The emphasis should not be placed on the requests but on God's faithfulness as the One who will provide for His people's needs.

By either interpretation, the verses are not meant for fulfilling unlimited self-centred requests, but always for God's glory. Nor are they meant as promises to fulfil all our prayers just as we pray them. As is true of the Sermon on the Mount, the verses must be seen as serving kingdom interests. Matthew 7:7–8 tells us that the gifts from God advocated in the Sermon on the Mount are available to everyone who asks, seeks and knocks. For example, Jesus said, 'Blessed are those who hunger and thirst for righteousness, for they will be filled' (Matt. 5:6, NRSV). He told a story about a tax collector who went to the Temple to pray. Unlike the Pharisee in the story, the tax collector stood at the rear and would not even look up to heaven. He beat his breast and said, 'God, have mercy on me, a sinner' (Luke 18:13). True to the beatitude, God answered the man's prayer. Jesus said, 'I tell you that this man, rather than the other, went home justified before God' (Luke 18:14).

2. Matthew 18:18–19 (see also 16:19). 'I tell you the truth, whatever you bind on earth will be bound in heaven, and whatever you loose on earth will be loosed in heaven. Again, I tell you that if two of you on earth agree about anything you ask for, it will be done for you by my Father in heaven.'

The only condition stated is that at least two people must agree about the request. Otherwise, the statement is starkly unqualified: 'Bind ... loose ... anything ... it will be done.'

Wilma is in heaven now, and Carl is alone. Last year Wilma died of breast cancer. They had served joyfully as missionaries in the Far East for 12 years. All during Wilma's illness the two of them had clung to Jesus' promise in Matthew 18:18–19, all to no avail. If ever a set of promises belonged to anyone, Wilma and Carl thought, they belonged to them. In the name of Jesus they 'bound' and 'loosed'.

Carl doesn't want to be a missionary any more. He is deeply puzzled – even disenchanted – over why Jesus' promises failed two missionaries who had freely answered God's call. How should we answer Carl regarding Matthew 18:18–19?

Explanation. First we should note the context (vv.15–20) in which the two verses occur. The subject of verses 15 to 20 is church discipline, not promises regarding prayer. The section anticipates a time when local congregations would exist, and it gives instruction regarding how discipline should be administered in the church.

According to verse 17, when an offending person does not listen to the group of two or three who have come to correct, the disciplinary matter should be brought to the attention of the church as a whole. If the offender refuses to repent, then he or she should be put out of the community.

In verse 18 the leaders of the community are given the authority to 'bind and loose'. The binding and loosing have to do directly with church discipline. Church leaders have the authority to make decisions regarding unrepentant sinners in the community. 'Loosing' means forgiving. 'Binding' means retaining the punishment.

The promise in verse 19 that has given Carl so much trouble should not have been claimed as a promise for Wilma. The strong promise is introduced to encourage the Church in its administration of church discipline. Because of the initial word 'again', we know that in verse 19 Jesus continues to address church discipline even as He did in the preceding verses. Jesus is also reiterating in verse 19 the substance of what he said in verse 18. Repetition was a common Hebrew way of stressing a point.

The Greek word for 'anything' means 'every matter', or every church problem that requires discipline. The church leaders must ask God for guidance. Where two or three of them agree regarding the appropriate course of action, they can be assured of God's guidance. What the disciples agree to on earth in disciplinary matters in the Church may also be taken as the will of heaven. The promise is that Christ Himself is acting along with the Church in matters of church discipline. The Church may count on assistance by the risen Christ

3. Matthew 21:22 (paralleled in Mark 11:12–24). 'Whatever you ask for in prayer with faith, you will receive' (NRSV).

What could possibly be clearer? Thelma asked this question as she listened to a preacher on television expound on Matthew 21:22. If ever God had spoken directly, she was sure she had heard His voice through the sermon. The preacher said, 'The promise is meant for every child of God. God is bound by His Word to honour His promise, with no reservations.'

So Thelma confidently claimed the promise. She believed that the little church she and her husband had supported for many years would not close. In faith believing, she and Roy – now virtually an invalid with rheumatoid arthritis – waited to see how God would save their church.

Two months ago the last family who could provide any financial support for the church moved to Dallas to find work, leaving Thelma and Roy alone on the Oklahoma plains. Two weeks ago the denominational official broke the bad news: the church would close. The once-thriving town had died.

The preacher on television would have served Thelma and Roy well if he had done more careful homework before preaching his sermon. Maybe he could have saved them from having serious reservations about God's faithfulness and worrying about where they went wrong. He had ripped the text out of its context.

Explanation. Verse 22 has to be placed within the context of verses 18 to 24. Matthew's version is shorter and simpler than that in Mark 11:12–24. The larger context of the

Matthew account is the passion narrative. In 20:17–19 Jesus foretells His death for the third time.

In 21:1–11 we hear of the events on Palm Sunday. In verse 12 Jesus enters Jerusalem, where He would be accepted by the blind and the lame but violently rejected by the Jewish authorities. Israel, in the form of those who controlled the religious establishment and who were politically influential, would reject Jesus. They would finally have Him nailed to a cross.

As we know, Jesus did not normally go around cursing fig trees. But on this particular morning, as He was returning to the city, He was hungry. He saw a fig tree by the roadside, went to it and found nothing. Then He cursed the tree: 'May you never bear fruit again!' (v.19).

As often happened, the disciples missed the point. They were amazed over how quickly the fig tree withered. They ignored the meaning of what Jesus had done. The fig tree is a symbol of Israel's religious barrenness. God came to Israel in the Person of Jesus, and Israel was not prepared to receive Him. Jeremiah 8:13 and Micah 7:1 use the fig tree as a symbol of Israel. Jeremiah speaks of Israel as a fruitless fig tree.

In spite of the disciples' rather irrelevant question about how Jesus could make the fig tree wither so quickly, Jesus honoured their question. So the subject changes from barren Israel to the faith that will keep the disciples from being powerless and barren like the fig tree. Israel's plight could, but didn't need to, become the disciples' failure also.

In an effort to teach, Jesus gave a short sermon on the importance of faith. Emphatically, Jesus told the disciples that as they serve Him in the kingdom, if they have faith, they will, for the kingdom's sake, do what many think impossible. Remember that Jesus is about to leave His disciples. He will entrust His ministry to them. He uses hyperbole (exaggerated speech) to make His point ('but even if you say to this mountain'). His words are meant for instruction, not for literal application.

Let's illustrate. If a mother says to her child, 'If I've told you once, I've told you a thousand times', she's using hyperbolic speech. What if the child sat down and began to count the 'one thousand times'? He or she wouldn't do it for long. Teachers often use hyperbolic speech. So did the rabbis. Jesus told Peter to forgive seventy-seven times (Matt. 18:22). He used exaggeration to say, 'Forgive until you've finally lost count. Forgiveness has nothing to do with calculations.'

Matthew 21:22 is part of what Jesus is trying to teach the disciples. Treating it out of context as an isolated promise abuses the Scriptures. Verse 22 is essentially connected to verses 18 to 21. Jesus' statement at once generalises and limits the point He's trying to make. 'Whatever' is limited by the words that follow: '... you ask in prayer.' This limits the granting of requests to the will of God. It is similar to Jesus' limiting words in John 14:13–14 and 16:23, 'in my name'.

In Matthew 21:22 Jesus doesn't offer His disciples magical power to do whatever they please or to perform marvellous feats – such as withering a fig tree – for their own sake. Jesus' promises regarding faith and prayer must be governed by the purposes of God He's now achieving. Indeed, individual needs and petitions are important and included in God's promises. But the text should not be misunderstood as an open account for fulfilling private interests unrelated to the larger will and kingdom of God. Prayer is Christian when governed by the criteria Jesus stated. 'Thy Kingdom come. Thy will be done, on earth as it is in heaven' (Matt. 6:10, KJV).

The promise in 21:22 deals primarily with the more serious and everyday matter of fruitfulness in the disciples. The verse has nothing to do with promising either the disciples or us that if only we have faith we will be able to do anything we want – perform any miracle or astound the world with wonders. This includes miracles that make good sense in terms of human need. The wonderful promise in verses 21 to 22 points to the miraculous power available to the disciples for fruitfully living the Christian life.

After Mark's account of the fig tree and Jesus' instructions regarding faith and prayer, Jesus warns us that we should not expect God to hear our prayers if we have not forgiven our neighbour (Mark 11:20–25).

THE LUKE TEXTS

1. Luke 11:5–13. 'Then he said to them, "Suppose one of you has a friend, and he goes to him at midnight and says, 'Friend, lend me three loaves of bread'"' (v.5).

Early in her life Sybil believed God had called her to the Christian ministry. Her minister, family and friends encouraged her. So she went to Bible college to prepare, hoping to become the pastor of a church. After graduation no doors opened. She had quickly hit a glass ceiling. While reading the Scriptures one morning, Luke 11:5–13 seemed to address her problem. She too believed that God would surely give to her what He had called her to do. She was sure God would be more responsive than the man who said to his neighbour, 'Don't bother me.' She knew her heavenly Father would give good gifts to her.

So Sybil went to the Lord in prayer. She asked and she knocked, but she did not find, did not receive. So she went on for further training as a hospital chaplain. Ten years after graduating, Sybil has not yet been offered a place of pastoral service. She now wonders about her call and the promises. Her confidence is waning.

Explanation. Luke 11:5–13 appears after Jesus has taught the disciples how to pray (the Lord's Prayer, 11:1–4). Only Luke preserves the parable. The verses present a striking contrast between a grouchy, reluctant 'friend' and our loving heavenly Father. The section moves us beyond the reluctant 'friend' who nevertheless assists his neighbour, to the heavenly Father, who quickly and willingly gives to His children 'fish' and 'eggs' instead of 'snakes' and 'scorpions'. He is anxious to give good gifts to His children.

The section takes us back to the 'Father' of the Lord's Prayer. Verses 5 to 13 actually form a commentary on the Lord's Prayer. The whole purpose of the parable is to lead us to the heavenly Father. It is supposed to encourage us to pray the Lord's Prayer with confidence. In accordance with the language of the Lord's Prayer, God will respond to our needs as we lay them before Him. Friends come through for us in spite of inconvenience. How much more will our heavenly Father come through for us?

Many Christians read these verses and conclude that the Father has offered an 'open and unlimited chequebook'. If anything, the heavenly Father seems to be indulgent, just the kind of Father who would say, 'You want it? You've got it.' Even the element of 'persistent asking' seems to be missing.

Verses 9–13 explicitly state the contrast between the 'friend' and the 'Father'. 'So I say to you: Ask and it will be given to you; seek and you will find; knock and the door will be opened to you' (v 9). God's greatness should not frighten us away from approaching Him. He isn't too busy running the universe to quickly respond to His children.

The Lord's Prayer says, 'Give us each day our daily bread' (v. 3). Verses 9 to 13 tell us how and in what measure God will answer our daily petitions. Not only will the Father respond, but He will give only good gifts to His children. The verses are meant to tell us what He is like, just as the Lord's Prayer has done. The disciples should be bold in their requests.

Those who see this text principally as promises for material things need to read more carefully. 'Daily bread' is certainly included in the promise. But the most important promise, that for which the children of the Father should long most, is the gift of the Holy Spirit.

The conclusion, 'How much more', is frequent in rabbinical literature. It accentuates the point that if something is true in a small instance, how much more will it be true in the larger case. If we, being evil, know how to give good gifts to our children, then 'how much more' will God give good gifts to His children! But the most important 'more' is the Holy Spirit, whom the Father will give to us. He is far greater than all earthly gifts.

We must not miss the point that the promises, though including material things, find their highest fulfilment in the gift of the Holy Spirit. The Spirit will make it possible for God's children to live as citizens in His kingdom. He will plant in them the life and power of the kingdom. For this, the children should rejoice most. The Spirit is the Father's highest gift. So why not request that gift above all others (see Rom. 15:13–19)?

Luke 11:5–13 presents an intimate picture of the relationship between God and His children. He urges us to approach Him in intimacy and with confidence. The verses must be firmly grounded in the Lord's Prayer, in which Jesus teaches His disciples the fundamental attitudes of prayer. *First,* they must have a concern for God's character and honour, and a desire to see Him overcome evil. *Second*, they must subject all their individual interests and petitions to an overriding desire for the kingdom of God to come on earth, even as it has come in heaven. *Third*, Jesus' disciples should guard God's honour and always pray in a way that His glory will be displayed to all. *Fourth*, in addition to, and more urgent than, requests for basic material provisions, Jesus' disciples should pray for forgiveness and spiritual protection. When asking for forgiveness, they are required to forgive others. Disciples who want to honour God will do so by the way they live – in dependence upon the Father.

2. Luke 18:1–8. 'Then Jesus told his disciples a parable to show them that they should always pray and not give up' (v.1).

Explanation. This parable and Jesus' explanation is one of the most difficult of all the texts of frustration. It is similar to Luke 11:5–13. It tells us that God will not delay long in helping His children who call upon Him. As in Luke 11:5–13, Jesus contrasts the willing God with a human who is reluctant to help those who call for assistance. But in this parable the contrast is even stronger. The figure with whom God is contrasted is not a reluctant friend, but 'a judge who neither feared God nor cared about men' (v.2).

Here is a man who is used to ignoring requests. One day a widow, a person with little or no political clout, came to the judge. She requested justice against someone who had wronged her. Being as he was, the judge had no inclination to pay attention to this woman who occupied a low rung on the social ladder. But she did not give up easily. She kept coming back again and again.

Finally, wearied by her persistence and recognising that she would not give up, the unjust judge caved in. He said, 'Give that woman whatever she wants. Anything to shut her up!'

In sharp contrast to the unjust judge, Jesus spoke of God who is both just and loving. 'And will not God bring about justice for his chosen ones, who cry out to him day and night? Will he keep putting them off? I tell you, he will see that they get justice' (18:7–8).

If ever words of Jesus should encourage Christians to expect God to act quickly and always to relieve the anguish of His people, here they are. If an unjust judge can finally be moved to execute justice, how much more faithfully and immediately will God act to relieve His people?

But we would have to be blind not to recognise that in instance after instance this simply does not happen. Early Christians died while being torn apart by wild animals in Roman arenas. Others were burned at the stake. Millions of Jews died in the Holocaust while awaiting divine deliverance. Just days before the Allies liberated his prison camp, the Nazis hanged Dietrich Bonhoeffer, thus ending the life of one of the world's most promising Christian leaders. This very day many Christians suffer – even die – because of their Christian witness. And, as we've discussed earlier, consider all those Christians who suffer physically and emotionally in our world, who plead for God to relieve their pain and He doesn't.

'And will not God grant justice to his chosen ones who cry to him day and night? Will he delay long in helping them? I tell you, he will quickly grant justice to them' (vv.7–8, NRSV).

What are we to say? The apparent contradiction between Jesus' words and what many Christians endure speaks for itself. We should dismiss two available explanations. One is that Jesus' use of the unjust judge in the parable encourages Christians to be tenacious when offering their petitions to God. They should 'storm heaven' in their persistence. But that's not what the text says. Jesus *contrasts* the willing heavenly Father with the wicked and resistant judge.

The other flawed explanation is that Jesus' promise is only for God's 'chosen ones'. All people who in true repentance and obedient faith confess Jesus to be the Christ *are* the children of the kingdom. The fact is that many of God's children call out to Him for help in desperate circumstances, but God does not 'quickly grant justice to them'. We can't get around this by dividing the Church into the 'elect' and the 'nonelect'.

Frankly, the commentaries don't resolve all the questions this text raises. But they do help.

E. Earle Ellis (*The Century Bible*) says Luke is apparently writing to a situation in which Christians are enduring severe persecution, a crisis in the Church. The persecution may be so great that some are denying their faith. The Christians are 'crying to God day and night' for relief from persecution.

Jesus' promise to His disciples should be understood as an eschatological (the completion of the kingdom, the last things) promise. This means that the text deals with the completion (fulfilment) of the kingdom at Christ's second coming. The suffering saints of God will be vindicated. The promises of God's speedy response are assurances to a persecuted Church regarding the second coming of Christ (the *parousia*). His coming is soon and His vindication will come with Him.

For much of the Early Church, the 'delay' of the second coming of Christ was not a chronological or temporal issue – it was a matter of life and death. For many of the young churches, waiting for the Lord to return and complete the kingdom meant they would have to endure more persecution. Many Christians would be imprisoned, martyred, or both. The Early Church, like some parts of the Church today, called out for the Lord's return within a context of intense persecution.

'Maranatha!' (Lord, come!) was no mere expression of casual interest or topic of abstract debate. It was a call for the Lord to vindicate His Church before its persecutors.

But the major concern was that the Lord would be revealed in His glory, not that Christians were dying. Most often Christians died as a remarkable testimony to the Lord and to their faith. Tertullian (c.AD 150–225) said, 'The blood of the martyrs becomes the seed of the Church.'

The text calls to mind words in the book of Revelation: '"See, I am coming soon; my reward is with me, to repay according to everyone's work. I am the Alpha and the Omega, the first and the last, the beginning and the end." ... The one who testifies to these things says, "Surely I am coming soon."' And John, on behalf of the Church, cries out, 'Amen. Come, Lord Jesus!' (22:12, 20, NRSV).

For some Christians the delay of the second coming, amid persecution and death, caused hope to fade and apostasy (departure from the faith) to increase. The book of Hebrews, for example, was probably written to a young Christian congregation facing intense persecution. Most of the congregation members were probably Jews who had embraced Christ as the Messiah. But now, in difficult times, many in the congregation were being tempted to return to Judaism. There are repeated exhortations to those whose faith is weakening (2:1; 10:32–36).

Interpreting this text of frustration within the context of the Early Church's persecution while anxiously awaiting the second coming is supported by Jesus' haunting question in Luke 18:8: 'However, when the Son of Man comes, will he find faith on the earth?'

So this text of frustration turns out to be the Church's cry for the Lord's return to vindicate the saints before an unbelieving and hostile world. And it is Christ's promise to the Church that He will not long delay. John Pollard says that the word 'quickly' does not mean 'immediate'. 'Quickly' has to do with the faithful character and promise of God. The Church can count on this, whatever the age or situation in which it exists. The Church, John Pollard says, should 'hang on to the "quickly"' (*Word Bible Commentary*). Others maintain that the Greek word means 'suddenly'.

Those who read this text correctly must do so as part of the universal Church of Jesus Christ that longs for the Lord's return. We must read the text in union with all the saints of God through the ages. We should understand Luke 18:1–8 in solidarity with both the Church Triumphant and the Church Militant. The text is for the Church, as the Church's longing for the Bridegroom to return.

One of the most stirring appeals for the Lord's return and the vindication of the saints appears in Revelation 6:9–10. When the Lamb opened the fifth seal, John saw under the altar the souls of those who had been slaughtered (martyred) for God's Word and for their testimony. They cried out, 'How long, Sovereign Lord, holy and true, until you judge the inhabitants of the earth and avenge our blood?' (v.10).

Indeed, we make individual appeals for help and vindication to the Lord. But Luke 18:1–8 is not principally about that. It is a loving and longing plea by Christ's Body around the world. We should often make the appeal Jesus invites us to make. But we should do so principally on behalf of all those in Christ's Church who, in order to bear witness to Him, must even today face the possibility of martyrdom.

THE JOHN TEXT

John 16:23–24. 'On that day you will ask nothing of me. Very truly, I tell you, if you ask anything of the Father in my name, he will give it to you. Until now you have not asked for anything in my name. Ask and you will receive, so that your joy may be complete' (NRSV).

We've left perhaps the most difficult text of frustration until last. What could be plainer or more straightforward than this? 'If you ask anything of the Father in my name, he will give it to you' (v.23)? Could we fault anyone who takes the Lord at His Word and asks confidently in His name? 'In my name' is the only limitation the text sets. It seems to urge Christians to petition the Lord for relief from all hindrances that keep them from thriving as Christian parents, spouses, pastors, laypeople, business people and so forth. A person simply needs to request 'in Jesus' name' and should confidently expect his or her prayers to be answered.

If success doesn't follow, obviously God has defaulted on His promise. Neither He nor we should be surprised if frustrated, disillusioned, and angry people are left behind.

A few years ago a pastor in Florida made such a promise to his congregation. He urged members to tithe on the basis of what, in the Lord's name, they wanted to earn as an annual income. The more the people earned, the more they could give to the church, he contended. A contractor followed the pastor's instructions and promptly went bankrupt. Angry and 'defrauded by God', the contractor sued the church, not being able to reach the Lord. But the judge threw the case out of court, saying he didn't know how to subpoena God.

Explanation. What help do the commentaries give us?

First, let's establish the larger context. This text forms part of Jesus' farewell discourse that runs from 14:1 to 17:26.

None of the other Gospels have anything quite like this. The farewell discourse provides an interpretation of Jesus' completed work on earth. It also teaches us the relation of the risen and glorified Christ to the believers (14:1–31), and the believers' relation to the world (16:1–33). We learn of the pattern of the Christian life in 15:1–27. Prominent in the farewell discourse is the promise of the Holy Spirit (14:2–17; 25–27; 16:4–15). After the farewell discourse comes Jesus' high-priestly prayer (17:1–26).

The text of frustration concerning us here is the part of the farewell discourse that teaches us what the Christian's relation to the world should be. In 16:16–24 Jesus teaches His disciples that the pain over His death will yield to joy because of His resurrection. It will lead to Christ's abiding presence through the promised Holy Spirit.

Verses 16 to 18 may refer more directly to Jesus' post-resurrection appearances (chaps. 20–21) than to the Holy Spirit's coming. At any rate, Jesus has already assured His disciples that He would not leave them as orphans (14:18). He would come to them in the Person of the Holy Spirit. Although for us, living on this side of Easter and Pentecost, all of Jesus' words seem clear, we have to put ourselves in the puzzled disciples' place. They had not seen the rest of the story when Jesus was speaking about leaving them.

So the tone of this text of frustration is Jesus reassuring His disciples as He is about to leave them. He is preparing these perplexed men for His death ('In a little while', 16:16) and for the good things that will follow. At first they will be like a woman in labour. But afterwards they will rejoice that a child has been born (vv.20–21). The disciples have pain now. But afterwards they will receive a joy that no one will be able to take away.

Then comes the promise that can be a source of frustration for faithful Christians: 'On that day you will ask nothing of me. Very truly, I tell you, if you ask anything of the Father in my name, he will give it to you. Until now you have not asked for anything in my name. Ask and you will receive, so that your joy may be complete' (vv.23–24, NRSV).

Given what Jesus has been trying to tell the disciples, 'on that day' refers primarily to the time after the resurrection, maybe to the time after Jesus has ascended and the Holy Spirit has been sent. Commentators are simply not sure what meaning we should give to 'ask nothing of me'. Does it mean 'you will ask me no questions' or 'you will ask me for nothing'? On the surface it seems to contradict the next sentence in which Jesus encourages the disciples to ask. 'Ask nothing' may mean don't 'ask a question' or don't 'ask for a gift'.

The best interpretation is that after the resurrection, the disciples would not need to ask for further information from Jesus. They would then have access to all the information they would need, because the Holy Spirit would be with them to teach them everything and to remind them of all that Jesus had said (14:26). Jesus had promised earlier that the Holy Spirit would guide the disciples into all truth (16:13).

'Very truly, I tell you', or 'I tell you the truth' usually introduces a new thought. It does not simply repeat an earlier idea. The 'asking' at the end of verse 23 appears to be different from the 'asking' at the beginning of the verse. But an alternative view is that the whole verse deals with prayer. If this is what verse 23 is about, then Jesus is saying that prayer will be directed to the Father and not to Him. In either case, the events that are about to occur will change everything.

After Jesus' resurrection, the disciples would not return to the same situation. In the future they would direct their prayers to the Father, who would give them 'whatever' they ask in Jesus' name. Jesus' promise sets no limit upon what the Father will give.

In verse 24 Jesus tells the disciples that a new state of affairs is about to begin. Until now the disciples have directly asked either Jesus or the Father for things. In Jesus' name they have asked nothing of the Father. That will change. Jesus tells the disciples to ask and to keep on asking. They will receive.

The purpose for all of this is the disciples' 'joy'. They will go through trials (v.33), but as they place their trust in God, He will place joy in their hearts. Joy is connected with prayer. The purpose for the disciples' prayer is that their joy may be made 'complete'. It can be made complete only through prayer.

The requests John has in mind are not primarily for the ordinary needs of life. They are for whatever will deepen eternal life and make the Holy Spirit's work fruitful. Both verses 23 and 25 show concern for a deeper understanding of Jesus through the Holy Spirit.

So all post-resurrection followers of Jesus should 'ask'. They have Jesus' guarantee that they will receive. But the promise is for gaining a deeper understanding of Jesus. That is the overriding Christian quest. The promise has nothing to do with wildly asking God to satisfy each desire or whim. The promise does not rule out material blessings and/or physical healing. But material blessings are not the principal intent or content of the promise. Those who refer to the text in this way mistreat it.

The fullness of Christian joy is what Christians should pray for. As they ask, they will receive (v.24) fullness of joy. The goal of Christian life has to do with coming to know Christ much better through the Holy Spirit.

CONCLUSION

The explanations of the scriptures we have examined were meant to clear up frustrating misunderstandings that the texts often suggest on the surface. I want to clarify that the explanations are not intended to deprive anyone of the right as God's child to take his or her petitions to Him in Christ's name. We are His children and He invites us into His heart. But we must be careful when using the Scriptures as bases for our petitions. We must study God's Word carefully and be guided by it.

The New Testament writers wrote with large purposes. To know what the New Testament says to us today regarding prayer or any other part of our faith, we must seek to understand the writers' larger purpose.

God's Word is the rich treasure of the Church. It is not locked away from us. But when appealing to God's Word for instruction, nourishment and correction, we should show the Bible proper respect by using study tools that will take us beyond superficial readings. Above all, even in our most careful study, we must ask the Holy Spirit to make the Bible the living Word of God. Even then, we will want to pray a prayer similar to this:

Almighty God, the fountain of all wisdom, who knowest our necessities before we ask and our ignorance in asking: Have compassion, we beseech thee, upon our infirmities, and those things which for our unworthiness we dare not, and for our blindness we cannot ask, mercifully give us for the worthiness of thy Son Jesus Christ our Lord, who liveth and reigneth with thee and the Holy Spirit, one God, now and for ever. *Amen*
(The Collect for the Seventh Sunday after Pentecost, *Book of Common Prayer*).

09

Prayer that words can't express

Abuong Malong and her three girls, all under 12, were fetching water when Arab slave traders thundered into Rumanlong. The raiders began shooting at the clusters of mud and wattle huts. Then they set Rumanlong on fire and began to kill the men in the village. They rounded up cows and goats. Abuong Malong and her three girls ran for the trees. Some of the raiders chased them. Although Abuong escaped, her three girls were captured.[1]

Along with the others who were captured, Abuong's three children were forced to carry the 'spoils' of the raid – sacks of grain – to Northern Sudan. There the captives would be sold to wealthy Arab families who owned farms and plantations near Darfur and Kordofan.

Each year these Arab families buy between 50 and 100 slaves. The female slaves perform farm and household tasks, as well as sexual services. If the women are young enough, they will be genitally mutilated when they reach puberty.

Abuong and her family – all of them Christians – had become victims of the civil strife now convulsing Sudan.

The government of Sudan denies that slave trading occurs. Southern Sudan is largely Christian. Northern Sudan is largely Muslim. Of the population, 70 per cent are Sunni Muslim, 25 per cent hold to indigenous beliefs and 5 per cent are Christians. The Christians are located south of Khartoum. The South is extremely poor and weak. The North is comparatively wealthy and strong.

After hiding until the slave traders and their captives had left, Abuong went back to her devastated village to search for her husband. She found him in what was left of their house with a bullet through his head. In a few short minutes Abuong's world had been shattered.

Now Abuong was alone. She faced poverty and bleaker destitution than she had known before. She has mentally relived countless times the events of four years ago. Since that horrible day, she has not seen her girls. She knows from slaves who have escaped what is probably happening to them. There's no reason to think she'll ever see them again.

Before her life was torn apart, Abuong was a Sunday School teacher. She taught Bible classes and was a person of prayer. Now, Abuong's unutterable anguish and fear suffocate her efforts to pray. She can do no more than mutter aborted sounds that start out as prayer and then fall back to the ground.

MARGARET

On the day before Margaret learned that Jeff, her husband, had multiple sclerosis, they both uncovered a dark secret. They had never understood why their 26-year-old son had never been able to achieve stability. He had wandered from one job to another, one friend to another, and one place of residence to another. Damon was bright and friendly. He made friends easily but could not focus his energies and talents on anything productive. He had struggled through college before finally graduating and had been employed by three firms; each of which showed promise of being a setting in which Damon could have succeeded.

Finally, Damon had asked to meet with his parents. For four hours he told Margaret and Jeff about repeated childhood sexual abuse he had suffered at the hand of a relative. The relative had baby-sat Damon while Margaret and Jeff were working away from home.

Now Margaret is suffering the deep anguish of Damon's fathomless pain, mistrust and confusion. She has also been staggered to her core by the news that her husband has rapidly advancing multiple sclerosis.

Margaret has always been a retiring person but a strong Christian. Prayer has been a major source of strength and growth. No more. Two years after Damon's revelation, with his struggling in counselling and Jeff becoming less mobile, Margaret is a beaten person. She knows all the words about victorious living. She has read books about how to pray. She has heard the sermons. But she is emotionally, physically and religiously exhausted. She and Jeff still attend church. But sometimes she wonders if she would do just as well to send a mannequin in her place.

She simply cannot pray. She has tried repeatedly. But words fall into senseless jumbles. To tell the truth, as far as she is concerned, God has gone into full eclipse. Margaret can only groan from some place too deep in her soul to explore.

If ever two people were lost in a religious jungle, Abuong and Margaret are exhibits 'A'. Pray? Call upon God in intercession? Offer petitions? They can't even formulate a coherent thought in prayer. They can't utter an intelligible sentence. Abuong and Margaret appear to be orbiting in different universes than the one God is in.

Maybe someday their circumstances will change. Who knows? Maybe one or more of Abuong's girls will escape. Maybe Damon will emerge from counselling and become a stable son. Maybe then Abuong and Margaret will reconnect with God. Perhaps, like Job, the good years will be restored. Until then, Abuong and Margaret live in spiritual wastelands, far from vibrant prayer and fellowship with God.

A friend of mine who also lives in such desolation speaks of 'pain without meaning'. His prayer each morning is simply, *Dear Jesus, You know who I am and what I'm going through. Please help me.*

THE GOD WHO PRAYS FOR US

Is this really the case? Can suffering be so religiously and psychologically debilitating that for some Christians effective prayer passes beyond reach? Can God, as Abuong and Margaret now feel, just pass out of sight? When they can't pray, when God seems remote, has He in fact abandoned them?

If so, we need to expose as a universal fraud what is called the 'Christian gospel'. If the horrors of life can place devastated Christians outside God's active and redemptive presence, then God has finally met His match, and Romans 8:31–39 is not true.

Does the New Testament offer anything that would prevent us from drawing this dark conclusion?

Yes!

As though the apostle had actually anticipated Abuong and Margaret, Paul penned some words to the Romans that voice the farthest possible reach of the gracious Father to His forlorn children. In these words, Paul plumbs the depths of prayer in a measure that taxes our comprehension. What he says can be received only as we understand the heart of the heavenly Father, who always remains faithful to His children. Paul's words soar into regions that transcend all human expectations. They would make little sense apart from Jesus' promises regarding the Holy Spirit's coming. He said the Spirit would be our advocate before the Father (John 16:4–11).

In Romans 8 Paul explains what it means to live in the Holy Spirit's power. Christians are to do this even though they live 'in the flesh'. Paul tells his readers how the Holy Spirit gives life to Christians, and speaks of the surpassing worth of the glory that will be revealed to Christians when Christ returns. He paints a majestic picture of just how broad the range of Christ's redemption will be. It will include creation as well as people.

Then all of a sudden Paul begins to speak of things that *groan* (Rom. 8:18–27). This may seem like a shift in mood and subject matter. In fact it isn't. Paul descends into the reality of suffering by Christians and suffering by creation. The sufferings about which Paul speaks reach such depths they succeed in taking hold of all the Abuongs and Margarets in the world.

Paul speaks of the 'sufferings of this present time' (Rom. 8:18). People who think the Christian gospel is superficial should reflect on Paul's unabridged realism. Remember that for Paul, suffering was far more than an abstract topic. He had suffered intensely. If you want to review some of the sufferings (beatings, imprisonment, shipwreck, rejection and so forth) he endured for the gospel, read Acts 12:24–28:22.

Paul uses the word 'groaning' to name *three* kinds of suffering. *First* he speaks of creation groaning. Obviously his language should be taken as metaphorical. Paul is articulating a profound, often overlooked, part of the Christian faith. Because people and evil powers employ nature for purposes contrary to God's will, creation 'longs' to be rid of the abuse. It longs to enter the *shalom* of God that is nature's birthright in Christ.

Paul says the creation's groaning is like a woman in labour. It is associated with the creation waiting for God's children to be revealed at the second coming of Christ. Creation also eagerly waits to be set free from its own bondage to decay. It will also obtain the freedom of the glory of God's children.

Maybe others have forgotten what God has in store for His creation. But creation hasn't forgotten. It knows that something's wrong with the way things currently are. But it also knows that its days of redemption are drawing near. It will obtain freedom. Now, however, the creation is going through 'labour'. Its suffering, its groaning, has nothing to do with futility or abandonment. It's like the groaning of anticipation a woman in labour experiences, even though accompanied by intense pain.

Second, Paul says we who are Christians, who have received the Holy Spirit, also *groan* deeply. The word Paul uses here is deep sighing, sighing inwardly. But again, this groaning has nothing to do with despair. Christians already have God's down payment, His promise that the kingdom of peace and justice Jesus established will be completed on earth. So we sigh deeply, we suffer, in anticipation of Christ completing His redemptive work – the 'redemption of our bodies'.

Contrary to repeated errors in the Church that indicate otherwise, Paul teaches that all we are, the whole person, will finally be redeemed. The Holy Spirit whom the Father has given to us is the down payment, the first fruit and the foretaste of things to come. The 'more' will look like what God has already given.

Creation groans. Christians groan. And next the apostle says that the Holy Spirit groans (Rom. 8:26, KJV). He groans before the Father in intercession. He intercedes before the Father *according to the will of God* (v.27). 'With groans that words cannot express.' The *American Standard Version* puts it, 'with groanings which cannot be uttered'. In John, Jesus says that teaching us what to say will mark the Holy Spirit's activity as our Advocate. Here we catch a glimpse of what Jesus' words meant. Not only does the Holy Spirit sometimes teach us what to say, but also in some instances He even says it for us. He formulates our words and thoughts when we can't do it for ourselves.

But why would the Holy Spirit groan 'with sighs too deep for words'? Can the eternal God groan? Is God so vulnerable that in the depths of His own existence He sighs as one who suffers? Does He, too, have groans too deep to express? What kind of God would this be? Can God really experience an inward sighing similar to the first two types of groaning?

That's precisely what Paul says. God suffers in the Person of the Holy Spirit. How can we expect to comprehend this? It's too high for us (Rom. 11:33–35). 'How unsearchable [are] his judgments' (v.33). Furthermore, Paul tells us that the Spirit searches the mind of God. When the Spirit groans in sighs too deep for words, He is plumbing the depths of our hearts and giving voice to our sighs in the Father's presence. He is accurately expressing our anguished pain. That's how firmly the eternal triune God has joined Himself to His people. 'Oh, the depth of the riches of the wisdom and knowledge of God!' (v.33).

Creation suffers. Christians suffer. Perhaps this much

we can understand. But a suffering, groaning, sighing God? Whoever heard of such a thing? Not the Greek philosopher Aristotle. For Aristotle such a God would be unworthy of the name. A suffering God would lose His own being in a minute.

But that's what the God who created the heavens and the earth does. He suffers; He groans; He takes upon Himself; He absorbs, carries and accepts the depths of human anguish.

What brings about the Holy Spirit's sufferings, His groaning? The inarticulate anguish of God's children who suffer, who are so uncertain about how they should pray, and who have suffered so immensely that they can't even voice a prayer.

But why does the Holy Spirit groan *intensely?* Because that's the measure of solidarity by which He prays for us. Pause now and be astonished by the Holy Spirit's groaning as He intercedes for us before the Father. The Holy Spirit bears our inarticulate sufferings, the tortured mumbles that spring from our grief or anguish. And then He prays for the Church! Amazing love!

The Spirit does this amid our weaknesses. He does it when we don't even know how to pray (Rom. 8:26). As on the Day of Pentecost, the Spirit is the great translator. He translates our groanings into language that can become an offering of praise and petition to the Father. The great Translator becomes our Advocate when we're too weak to express faith and hope.

God's groaning for us has another dimension. The context of the Romans text is important. The suffering creation and the suffering Church groan *in hope*. They hope the evil that mars God's creation will end. The groans express confidence that 'he who has come will come' to complete His kingdom on earth. Many times the Church asks, *How long, O Lord? How long? How long must mothers watch their children snatched away into slavery, their husbands killed, and their children sexually abused?*

How long will nations be in conflict, the innocent be victimised, and depression ravage one's spirit? How long, O Lord, will disease rack the body and soul, injustice go unpunished, and requests for relief go unrequited? How long, O Lord, How long? (Rev. 6:10).

At times God's children have been tempted to think He in His lofty security doesn't hear, is impassive or is too busy doing other things. The story of the 'groaning God' should forever end such suspicions. The text clarifies that 'groaning' isn't something God schedules once in a while. He does it whenever His people suffer, whenever their inarticulate groans escape their tortured souls. And that must mean *always*.

There's another dimension to God's vulnerability, to His groaning, that none of us can comprehend. If God is God, and if He sees how the world and His people suffer even more clearly than we do, then why doesn't He act now to consummate the kingdom of God? *We don't know.* The Church has never known. In the 'tarrying' of the Lord, the Church's faith is probably put to its greatest test and also given opportunity to rise to its highest achievement.

So far in our discussion of the creation that groans, the Church that groans, the Spirit that groans and the Father that groans, we've left out the foundation. All the sufferings and hope rest upon *the sufferings of our Redeemer*. He took upon Himself the form of a servant and became obedient, even to death on the cross (Phil. 2:7–8). He is the One who, on the cross, took upon Himself the sufferings of the world. 'In bringing many sons to glory, it was fitting that God, for whom and through whom everything exists, should make the author of their salvation perfect through suffering' (Heb. 2:10). Our Lord, by His shed blood, has won redemption for God's whole creation.

'Worthy is the Lamb, who was slain, to receive power and wealth and wisdom and strength and honour and glory and praise!' (Rev. 5:12). 'You were slaughtered and by your blood you ransomed for God saints from every tribe and language and people and nation; you have made them to be a kingdom and priests serving our God, and they will reign on earth' (Rev. 5:9–10, NRSV).

Nowhere in the New Testament does the covenant bond between Christ and His Church rise higher, and at no point does the covenant descend more into the depths.

Are Abuong and Margaret abandoned by God? Never. In prayer, must God's children achieve a high level of performance and refined speech before God will hear them? No. Even if God's children can't voice a coherent word, prayer is still happening. Because of the Holy Spirit, for the children of God, God is never distant.

CONCLUSION

In 1906 a race riot occurred in Atlanta, USA. Afterwards, W.E.B. DuBois wrote his famous piece, 'A Litany at Atlanta'. DuBois was sick of violence in all forms and from all quarters. His deeply-troubled faith is what we should hear: 'Bewildered we are, and passion-tossed, mad with the madness of a mobbed and mocked and murdered people; straining at the armposts of Thy Throne, we raise our shackled hands and charge Thee, God, by the bones of our stolen fathers, by the tears of our dead mothers, by the very blood of Thy crucified Christ: *What meaneth this?* Tell us the plan; give us the Sign!'

Then DuBois calls out, 'Whisper – speak – call, great God, for Thy silence is white terror to our hearts! The way, O God, show us the way and point us the path.'[2] *Silence. Silence?* Can we not hear in Dubois's lament both the human and the divine groans? They journey together.

10

Prayer at the end of life

Ivan Illich is dying, probably of pancreatic cancer. Five different physicians have offered little assistance. His family has lost patience with his suffering and tends to blame him for his illness. Gerasim, the family's servant, assists Ivan in his most basic needs. Gerasim is the only one who offers compassion to Ivan, a thoughtless and selfish man.

In *The Death of Ivan Illich*, author Leo Tolstoy powerfully shows how the imminence of death can force us to confront our own histories and mortality. As Ivan's condition worsens, he stops looking for ways to avoid the certainty of his death. He struggles to confront his own selfishness and desperate efforts to live. Ivan's wife and daughter mirror his selfishness and the way he lived before his illness.

Religious in only the most incidental sense possible, Ivan, at his wife's encouragement, turns to a priest and receives the sacrament of the Lord's Supper. He'll try anything.

Finally, exhausted, Ivan is in a position to hear from God. This had never occurred during his life as a judge in the Russian justice system. In a strikingly sober interchange between God and Ivan, God asks, 'What do you want?'

Ivan answers, 'I want to live.'

God responds, 'And what does it mean to live?'

Ivan could not give God a good answer.

Ivan Illich wanted to live. But his life had been missing depth, love, community, real friendship, faith and moral bearing. 'Life' for him had meant parties by which to impress people, plus card games, professional appointments, prestige and the best furniture, clothes, social contacts and the like. At the close, he admitted to himself that he had never truly lived.

The irony of the story is that the death of Ivan Illich opened the door for him to live. In the closing hours Ivan falls into a 'death' to his old self, and doing so leads to life. 'He fell through the hole and there at the bottom was a light. Ivan Illich fell through and caught sight of the light. For two more hours he suffered. Then something rattled in his throat, his emaciated body twitched, then the gasping and rattle became less and less frequent. "It is finished!" said someone near him. He heard these words and repeated them in his soul. "Death is finished," he said to himself. "It is no more!" He drew in a breath, stopped in the midst of a sigh, stretched out, and died.'[1]

THE DESIRE TO LIVE

Many who have seldom prayed will begin to petition God when they face death. Like Ivan Illich, they 'want to live'. Then for them, as for Ivan, God may raise the question, 'What is life?'

For Christians, as for Ivan, the question 'What does it mean to live?' is also appropriate.

There appears to be an interesting contradiction in the Christian request to live rather than die. On one hand,

Christians often say they long to go to heaven so they can be with the Lord. On the other hand, when Christians have an opportunity, through death, to go to heaven, they usually storm heaven with petitions to continue living. They park in the consultant's surgery and hospital and pursue promising remedies, hoping their life on earth will be extended.

One elderly Christian listened to a young minister waxing eloquent about the glories of heaven. After listening for half an hour, the man stood, picked up his cane, and announced, 'Any of you who wants it can have my ticket!' Then he left.

The fact is that most Christians want to live. If we were to encounter a Christian begging for an opportunity to die, we would quickly label that person morbid.

If Christians really want to go to heaven, should they petition God to live? If life after death with Christ is so desirable, why would Christians cling to life? If heaven is such a friend, why is death such an enemy?

WHAT CHRISTIANS BELIEVE ABOUT LIFE IN THE WORLD

How do Christians justify the petitions for life they present to God when death seems imminent? How can they justify their prayer to live instead of die?

These questions have good answers. There's also a good answer for the apparent conflict between viewing heaven as a friend but death as an enemy. Let's explore the answers.

First, Christians believe human life is God's gift and that it's good. The Old and New Testaments contain and celebrate the rich aspects of life. Domestic life with all its challenges and rewards is there. Music, merriment and dance appear often in the Old Testament. A wealth of instruction in worship, prayer and faith is included. Romance and marriage, friendship and conflicts, successes and failures, how to live in community, how to live justly and peaceably – all of these populate the Scriptures.

Poetry, history, political commentary, rich differences in literature and literary style – all can be found in God's Word. The stories of saints and rogues, the great and the small, the wise and the foolish, the rich and the poor – all of them take centre stage at one time or another. The Bible displays every sentiment known to humanity, both noble and scandalous.

The Bible celebrates life as God's good gift.

One thing that strikes a reader of the Bible is its 'earth-liness'. The Bible assumes that this earth is an appropriate place to know God and to walk with Him. Here on this planet, God intends that people explore what it means to be created in His image. Even though sin and evil plague the world, nowhere does the Bible say this world came about because some evil being created it or because God made a mistake. God made the world and called it good. It depends upon Him for its origin, continuation and future.

The Hebrews and Christians knew the world came to existence solely through God's action. 'This what God the LORD says – he who created the heavens and stretched them out, who spread out the earth and and all that comes out of it, who gives breath to its people, and life to those who walk on it: I, the LORD ...' (Isa. 42:5–6). From Revelation comes this doxology: 'You are worthy, our Lord and God, to receive glory and honour and power, for you created all things, and by your will they were created and have their being' (4:11).

The world isn't an enemy that God must overcome to prove He is God. In fact, this world is a place where even God feels at home, and why not? One cannot read very far into God's Word without being struck by how near He is to the world. Its existence doesn't threaten Him. In fact, God regularly gets all mixed up in the affairs of nations, families, individuals, and even nature's activity.

Second, the Bible tells us nothing created should ever be given the importance that belongs to God alone. Only He should be worshipped. We should live in the creation, enjoying and cultivating it. We can even use parts of it to glorify God – for example, sound turned into music. If treated any other way, if parts of it are worshipped, the world becomes unbalanced.

The Bible presents a sorry record of nations and individuals who have treated nature as deity. The prophets never stopped asking, 'Why would people whom God created fall down and worship other things that God created? Why would people worship idols instead of worshipping God?' Isaiah asked those who worshipped idols, 'To whom, then, will you compare God? What image will you compare him to? As for an idol ...' (Isa. 40:18–19).

A person conditioned by the Bible's affirmation of creation might take all of this for granted. Isn't it this way everywhere in all religions? No, some religions teach that the world is inherently evil. Others teach it is illusory and that we shouldn't give it much importance. Still other religions worship parts of the creation as gods. The apostle Paul said that people who worship creation become 'futile in their thinking'. They 'exchanged the glory of the immortal God for images made to look like mortal man and birds and animals and reptiles' (Rom. 1:21, 23).

CHRISTIAN PRAYER AT THE END OF LIFE

What we believe about God's relationship and our relationship to the creation has a direct bearing on how we live, pray and die. Christians should live and die in ways that grow directly out of their faith. What the Christian faith teaches regarding how we should value life and the world differs from what Buddhists, Hindus, Muslims, other religions and pagans teach. We Christians need to be sure that the way we view life in the world and how we pray when life in this world is ending shows that we're Christians and not pagans. A person can profess to be a Christian and still be fundamentally guided by pagan values.

Because of what Christians believe about God and His relation to creation, *Christians should want to live*. No one should celebrate life more than a Christian. Without ignoring the grief and tragedy in which millions of people live, life on earth should still be meaningful and desirable. That's the way God wants it. If this were not so, the Bible's insistence that we pursue peace, mercy and justice on earth would make no sense at all.

The Christian desire to live is rooted in the Old Testament. For the Hebrews, people were not seen as eternal souls living in insignificant animated shells. The Hebrews didn't think of people as divided into neatly segregated compartments the way Plato did. Nor did they think of the self as an illusion as the Buddhists do. They believed God created the whole person. They viewed the person as a whole, productively integrated into his or her environment. The land, for the Hebrews, was far more than geography – it formed the context for meaningful life.

Israel was supposed to be different from the other nations. Because of what the Jews believed about God and His relationship to the world, they were supposed to see people as having been created and sustained by God. The environment, family, history, geography, cities, employment, food and worship all played essential roles. Even the floods clapped their hands, and the hills sang in the Lord's presence (Psa. 98:8-9). And *meaning* included all of these. Meaningful life involved worshipping God in the way we live in His creation. Viewing life as meaningful and desirable was simply a way of worshipping God as Creator. No one could have a higher estimate of life than that.

The Christian valuation of life is consistent with that of the Hebrews. From a Christian perspective, wanting to live means affirming the Creator and the creation as His alone. Living meaningfully in the world is one way we express our faith and worship. It's consistent with Paul's charge to the Roman Christians: '... offer your bodies as living sacrifices, holy and pleasing to God – this is your spiritual act of worship' (Rom. 12:1). By living meaningfully, we also recognise our stewardship for God's world.

As we live this way in God's creation, meaning can increase. Life is the Christian's opportunity to celebrate God's good gifts – the gifts of His presence, occupations, family, friends and so forth.

WHY CHRISTIANS CAN LIVE AND DIE

Christians can live. They should live as robust witnesses to the Creator and Redeemer God. A minimal, escapist, negative and depreciatory approach to life may fit some religions, but not Christianity. Read about Jesus' life. What would we have seen if we could have trailed Him for a few days? A hermit? Someone who acted as if the everyday affairs of life are a sorry setting for human fulfilment? Read the New Testament and see how many times Jesus either attended parties and banquets, talked about them or promised them to His disciples.

No one accused Jesus of being a social recluse. But some people did contrast Him to John the Baptist, whom they preferred. Some of His critics said, 'Here is a glutton and a drunkard, a friend of tax collectors and "sinners"' (Luke 7:34). How Christians live should tell others about the kind of God they serve, about His creation and about their faith in Him.

Christians can die. Death is a part of life. That sounds obvious. But if the way we live shows what we believe about God, life and the world, then so does the way we die. We Christians should bear witness to Christ in how we die. In the way we die, we should demonstrate our hope of the resurrection.

But because we love life as God intended, and because we see this world as the place of divine visitation, we oppose death as an enemy. We *can die,* but we *want to live.*

There are at least two major types of contrasts to the way Christians should face death. Greek philosopher Socrates (c.470–399 BC) represents the first type. The Athenian Senate sentenced him to death by drinking a tea made from hemlock. Before Socrates died, his disciples grieved. He told them their grief showed their ignorance of what is most important about people. The soul is the permanent and meaningful part of a person, he said. The body with its emotions, hungers, weaknesses and needs is just a passing, animated shell. We will be much better off when at death the soul is set free to return to its source. Socrates said that people who see death as an enemy place too much emphasis on 'bodily pleasures and adornments' (*Phaedo* 114.e).

By contrast, those who have lived a life of 'surpassing

holiness' do not see death as an enemy. They know when they die their souls will live 'altogether without bodies, and [will] reach habitations even more beautiful, which is not easy to portray' (*Phaedo* 114.c).

When the time came for Socrates to drain the cup of hemlock, he 'received it quite cheerfully' (*Phaedo* 114.c–118).

The second contrast to the way Christians should face death appears in people who believe this physical life is all there is. Unlike Socrates, people who represent the second type think that when people die they come to a complete end. When breath flees, all is over. So these people cling to life at all costs. They wring from it every drop of biological and sensual activity they can. No cost for maintaining their meagre hold on existence is too great, for after this life nothing is left, they contend.

The apostle Paul said these people think the best approach to life is 'Let us eat and drink, for tomorrow we die' (1 Cor. 15:32). The contemporary version of this philosophy is 'You go around only once, so grab all you can'. These people fight against death's approach with all they have – because they think physical life is *all* there is.

Do either of these options match how Christians should approach death?

Some Christians speak and act more like Socrates than like Christians. They say that the soul is the only important part of a person, so they look forward to the time when the 'soul' will be set free from the body that weighs it down. The physical, earthly, social and emotional dimensions of life should forever be put behind. These Christians think the soul is the only part of the person to which salvation and hope apply. They live and die more like Socrates than like Christians, who should affirm the whole person as God's creation and His object of redemption.

Other Christians act as though the second approach to death is how Christians should face death. As they face death, they bargain with God. They cajole Him. In panic, they act and pray as though they were the universe's centre. Functionally, they act as if we have hope only in this life (1 Cor. 15:19). Prayer is extremely important for these Christians. But it is not the prayer of peace and trust.

If neither of these options is a Christian way to face death, what is?

Contrast these types with the outlook Paul gave to Christians in Corinth: 'This perishable body must put on imperishability, and this mortal body must put on immortality. When this perishable body puts on imperishability, and this mortal body puts on immortality, then the saying that is written will be fulfilled: "Death has been swallowed up in victory." "Where, O death, is your victory? Where, O death, is your sting?" The sting of death is sin, and the power of sin is the law. But thanks be to God, who gives us the victory through our Lord Jesus Christ' (1 Cor. 15:53–57, NRSV).

Socrates thought the 'holy' person should see death as a friend. Paul saw death as an enemy, the final enemy. 'The last enemy to be destroyed is death,' he wrote in 1 Corinthians 15:26.

Death is an enemy? Are people such as Socrates more brave and noble than Christians? Without doubt, Socrates would have reprimanded Paul.

Why the difference between Socrates and Paul? It goes back to a Christian understanding of creation and meaning. The apostle Paul was grounded in the Hebrew and Christian understanding of creation and meaning. He possessed the 'earthliness' we spoke of earlier. By contrast, Socrates thought the physical and emotional part of the person will drop away forever, with nothing lost. Good riddance!

But for Paul, the historical, physical, social, domestic and emotional dimensions of life are as much a part of God's good creation as is anything else. This fleshly world is where God chose to become incarnate. In this world – God's creation – the Son of God took upon Himself the form of a servant. Being found in human likeness, He 'became obedient to death' (Phil. 2:8). This world is the place where God sent His own Son in the form of sinful flesh (Rom. 8:3). This is God's creation, a fit place for human habitation. Right here Christians can live in the power of the Holy Spirit (vv.1–8).

Unlike Socrates, the apostle Paul believed the *whole person* is targeted for redemption. He believed this because he knew how 'fearfully and wonderfully' God has made us (Psa. 139:14). He knew that if Christ was truly successful, then no part of God's creation will be abandoned.

This is why Paul calls death an enemy. Death appears to put an end to meaning. It really does *disrupt* meaning, and if it were not for Christ's resurrection, death could completely destroy meaning. Death *is* an enemy. It leaves children without their mothers and fathers. It disrupts communities, families and friendships. Death cuts short careers in medical research, service in Christian ministry, and it takes away caregivers for elderly parents and children who have special needs. It deprives us of people we love. Death even has a way of doing this many times when 'meaning' is just beginning to bud in children.

That's why Paul called death an enemy. It even seemed to separate Christ from His Father. It seems to terminate meaning for all of us at one time or another. But the Christian hope of the resurrection assures us that life, not death, will have the final word. The One who is the Resurrection and the Life will speak last. He will speak the word of the resurrection!

A Christian love for life has nothing to do with treating this world as if it were a god. Christians don't 'love life' like pagans who think there's nothing more. But neither do they scorn historical, domestic, physical and emotional life as an ugly shell the soul must escape. A Christian love for life is a robust expression of faith in God the Creator. It is complete trust that all that's meaningful and loving is the object of redemption. Life should be a 'Hallelujah!' affirmation that we who belong to Christ will be 'made alive' in Him (1 Cor. 15:22). A Christian love for life is a lively 'Amen!' to the promise that 'the trumpet will sound, the dead will be raised imperishable, and we will be changed. For the perishable must clothe itself with the imperishable, and the mortal with immortality' (vv.52–53).

O Lord, let not the uncertainty of the future dismay me, or the lurking shadows bring me to despair; but with the lamp of hope burning brightly, may I complete my long pilgrimage, and at last come to the glories of the perfect day; through Jesus Christ our Lord. Amen.[2]

QUESTIONS REGARDING PRAYERS AT THE END OF LIFE

1. What should Christians request when they pray for those who are dying?

Most of us are uncertain about how we should pray for those who are terminally ill. Our uncertainty is understandable. We want to be helpful. We want to communicate our sorrow to the person facing death and to his or her family. On behalf of the dying person, we want God to do all that His will permits.

At the same time, we recognise medical diagnoses that point to imminent death. So how are we to pray for a friend or family member who is in the final stages of cancer? How do we pray for the diabetic for whom dialysis has lost its effectiveness?

First, we pray that the peace of the resurrected Christ will be upon them. That is the healing for which we should always pray. We can always be sure this prayer will be answered.

It is a pagan error to think the greatest need of a dying person is a physical one. As a brother or sister in Christ, or as a family member, we pray that the *shalom* of Christ will cover and enfold the terminally ill person. The peace of Christ is the presence of Christ. In the broadest sense, it is His salvation, His love. In intercession and in solidarity we pray that the dying person will be drawn near to the bleeding side of Jesus and to the loving heart of God. To pray the peace of Christ is to pray that the person will be assured that nothing, death included, will be able to separate him or her from the love of God in Christ Jesus our Lord (Rom. 8:31–39). Even if the person is not conscious, we pray the peace of Christ anyway.

Second, we may pray for physical healing. Through our intercession, God may act to restore health even to a dying person. Many are such testimonies, and we should always be prepared in faith to receive the grace of physical healing. This is not an encouragement to bargain with God or to act foolishly. It's a simple request: 'If you will ... Nevertheless, your will be done.'

At the same time we should pray that God will help the person and us to receive the grace to die. The grace to die is the gift that makes it possible to release our terminal lives into the care of the Redeemer, whom to know is life eternal. The grace to die is the grace that permits us to place our failures and our successes in God's keeping. It is a certainty that physical death can never interrupt fellowship with Him who was dead, whom God raised up by His mighty power and who is alive forevermore.

The grace to die is the confidence that because He lives, we will live also. It is receiving the assurance, "'I am the Alpha and the Omega,' says the Lord God, 'who is, and who was, and who is to come, the Almighty'" (Rev. 1:8). In this spirit and confidence Christians in terminal circumstances can pray for their own death:

O God, who art our refuge and our strength, and as the shadow of a great rock in a weary land, help me living and dying to yield myself to thee in faith and love. All along life's journey thou hast led me when I would reach out to touch thy hand; thou wilt not forsake me now. Go with me into the dark and on beyond to the glorious brightness of thine eternity.

For Jesus Christ our Lord, I give thee thanks above all earthly mercies. To him I pledge my loyalty and devotion to thy service, that I may be used as thou wilt for the forwarding of thy kingdom. In his name I pray. Amen. [3]

2. Should Christians ever pray for another's death?

As strange as it may seem, the answer is yes. With the revolution in our ability to sustain physical life far beyond any hope of meaningful recovery, this question's urgency and practicality increases. In many instances the only thing keeping a loved one alive is artificial hydration and respiration. Were it not for the artificial aids, the person would be dead. Prospects for meaningful recovery may be nonexistent.

But in most instances, neither the health care professionals nor the family can simply disconnect life-support systems. So we wait through what may seem like a pointless eternity.

In such instances a person who loves the dying individual can offer as a Christian prayer, *Lord, take her. Take her now into Your care and keeping. Help her now give back to You the life You gave to her.* Such a prayer is not selfish. But the one who prays – a minister, for example – may be aware that the prolonged illness from which this person will probably not recover has placed extreme strains on a family's resources. Considering this knowledge is not wrong.

3. Should Christians stop praying for one who is dying?

Many of us have reached a point, while being with a relative or friend who is dying, when we ask, 'Should we stop praying?' One answer is that we should never stop praying. But we may change the focus of our prayers. We may stop praying for healing and begin to pray that God would help him or her and us face death in a truly Christian way.

Claude Thompson, a theologian and professor at Emory University in the 1960s and early 1970s, died of cancer. Mrs Thompson reached a point at which she stopped praying for Dr Thompson's healing and began to pray that God would fill their remaining days together. She also prayed that God would prepare both of them for his death. God heard her prayer.

On the day of Dr Thompson's funeral in Emory Chapel, the congregation sang songs of Christian affirmation and hope. At the close of the service, as Mrs Thompson left the church, everyone could see by the look on her face that the Holy Spirit was helping her draw freely upon the Christ who had promised never to leave or forsake her.

4. How should Christians pray after God 'fails' to heal?

Perhaps we've asked God to heal a family member, a friend or a leader, and the petition was not granted. We may have prayed for years for someone's healing. We may have even thought God would heal the person. Sometimes this happens. But in other instances the person is not healed. How should we respond, and how are we to interpret this 'failure'?

As stated earlier, the apostle Paul exclaimed, 'How unsearchable are [God's] judgments and how inscrutable his ways!' (Rom. 11:33, NRSV). After that, there's nothing more to be said. No one knows why God chooses to grant physical or psychological healing in one instance but not in another.

For me, the book of James has always added to the puzzle: 'Is any one of you sick? He should call the elders of the church to pray over him and anoint him with oil in the name of the Lord. And the prayer offered in faith will make the sick person well; the Lord will raise him up' (5:14–15). Often these instructions have been followed, but the person for whom prayer was offered died. The Lord God did not 'raise him up'. Perhaps all of us have seen people try to cajole, even reprimand God when prayers are not answered as desired. I have seen instances in which Christians speak so immaturely in their petitions that they fall into 'unbelief'.

We're always supposed to do one thing, however, whether in response to healing or 'failure' to heal. We are to sing out the following doxology: 'For from him and through him and to him are all things. To him be the glory forever! Amen' (Rom. 11:36).

Whether God heals or does not heal should have no bearing on whether we worship Him with all our hearts. Again these words of determined faith from Habakkuk: 'Though the fig-tree does not bud and there are no grapes on the vines ... yet I will rejoice in the LORD, I will be joyful in God my Saviour. The Sovereign LORD is my strength ...' (3:17–19).

O Lord, support us all the day long, until the shadows lengthen and the evening comes, and the busy world is hushed, and the fever of my life is over, and our work is done. Then in thy mercy grant us a safe lodging, and a holy rest, and peace at the last. Amen.[4]

5. How should we pray for terminally ill children?

As hard as it is to absorb an adult's death, perhaps watching a child suffer is far more difficult. We're struck by the fact that death will shatter all potential. Before the child can explore the rich gift God has given, death takes him or her. Often cancer or liver disease has stalked the child for months, leaving the little one but a shadow of their former delight in life. The senselessness of a young life being prematurely ended can be overwhelming, suffocating.

The following part of a poem written by the mother of a child who died by sudden infant death syndrome expresses this sentiment:

I do not mourn you for what you were
But for what can't be
The unfinished life we didn't share.
The very briefness of that life
Has reached this day and makes me pause and know
I miss you[5]

How should we pray? We pray by embodying and expressing the grace, compassion and love of God. For a terminally ill child, this is no time for a public wrestling match with God. It is, however, a time when in actions and words we ask God to help us explain that the child's death doesn't spring from meanness, insensitivity or a failure of love on God's part. This is a time to speak often to the child regarding God's presence, of how Jesus received children and about His love for the child. It is also a time for explaining the child's disease to him or her.

Pray that God will give the caregivers strength, that their trust in God will increase, and that others will be drawn to Christ by the way we respond to the fatal illness.

Pray that God will empower the parents to place God's gift to them back in the hands of the gift-giver. Pray that God will make it possible for parents to love and worship the Lord of life.

When our youngest daughter was 18 months old she contracted spinal meningitis. When she was admitted to the hospital, we were told that this stiff, very sick child might not live through the night. God's promise was 'My presence will be with you.' We knew that what we had believed about trusting God was being tested. We prayed, 'God, she's Yours. We've done all we can. We're tired. Please let us sleep.' We slept through the night.

Abide with us now, O Lord, for it is toward evening and the day is far spent. O thou who neither slumbers nor sleepest, evermore be with thy children. As thou coverest the earth with darkness, cover us with thine infinite mercy; through Jesus Christ our Lord. Amen.[6]

11

The God beyond 'god'

A SUBSTITUTE JESUS

The twentieth-century American writer who probably did most to expose the folly of secularised and superficial Christianity was Flannery O'Connor. She was a Roman Catholic layperson who lived in Milledgeville, Georgia. Socially odd, even grotesque characters pass through her novels and short stories. She used these figures to show that people who struggle with Jesus' radical conditions for discipleship or who even try to reject the gospel, are much closer to the kingdom of God than those who try to waltz in without even 'breaking a sweat'. She did through fiction what Dietrich Bonhoeffer, the German Christian, did through theology. Both of them insisted that 'the call to discipleship is the call to come and die'.

In O'Connor's stories, socially ugly people enter the kingdom, while 'beautiful' people who believe they have the gospel under social control are left out.

'All my stories,' O'Connor wrote, 'are about the action of grace on a character who is not very willing to support it.'[1]

WHEN 'GODS' TRY TO BE GOD

Flannery O'Connor hoped she could help people become anchored in the God beyond 'god'. She knew that many of us sometimes fall victim to functionally reducing God to the size of a god. A strange character named Hazel Motes dominates *Wise Blood,* one of O'Connor's novels. Hazel wants to start a 'church without Jesus Christ'. After he had announced that he needed a new kind of 'jesus' for his church, one that didn't have to redeem people by his blood, Hazel set out to bring this new 'jesus' to them. The substitute 'jesus' turned out to be a mummy, stolen from the local museum. But the substitute 'jesus' was of no value at all. Accidentally soaked by rain, the substitute 'jesus' burst open and had to be thrown out of the back door.

The fact is that unless we are diligent we, too, can create a substitute 'jesus'. But any god we substitute for God will finally burst open and will have to be thrown out. Calling out in prayer to substitute gods will always lead to failure, disenchantment and confusion.

We can wish that it were not so, but each of us is tempted to create gods in our own image. We bear marks of humanity's fall. All too easily we forget we have finite minds, perspectives and interests. We're profoundly limited in our geographical, gender, economic, racial, national and social locations.

A story is told of a 'scholarly frog' who lived at the bottom of a well. Based on what he observed at the bottom of his well, the scholarly frog wrote an authoritative three-volume analysis of the ocean. Like the frog, we too easily think our own range of knowledge represents all there is to see. We tend to convert our own finitely limited locations into godlike perspectives on everything. We forget our limited evaluations, weaknesses and errors. Jesus exposed this tendency in His reference to those who can see the splinter in their neighbour's eye but can't see the log in their own eye (Matt. 7:1–5). Until the day we're taken home to heaven, we'll face the temptation to create gods in our own image. Yielding to this temptation leads to the sin of idolatry. Denial or ignorance of the temptation is one first step towards the sin itself.

Flannery O'Connor and others have called Christians to discern carefully between a 'gospel' that yields 'a church without Jesus Christ' and that gospel that leads us to confess with Peter, 'Lord, to whom shall we go? You have the words of eternal life' (John 6:68).

Things that merely exist have all the marks we associate with finite things. Time and space limit them. Their existence always depends on something or someone outside them. They are necessarily flawed and endangered, flimsy and passing. Even the mighty stars eventually use up all of their energy, and the mountains wear down to become plains.

If we try to make 'existing things', no matter how big, carry God's weight, they will fail. The Christians who reach maturity and a sure knowledge of God intentionally press beyond the gods that exist, to the God who doesn't bear the marks of finite things. 'I am the LORD; that is my name! I will not give my glory to another or my praise to idols' (Isa. 42:8).

However, no one ever gets beyond the temptation to reduce God to one of the gods. Moving beyond the gods is something we must choose to do again as each challenge emerges. For example, the temptation to pray to a god who has been reduced to the size of a nation, physical health or professional accomplishments, can ambush any of us. We must rely upon the Holy Spirit to lift us above the 'gods' and to ground us in the God who *is*. As J.B. Phillips put it, too often 'our God is too small'. Our God becomes too small when the range of our prayers is reduced to our physical and material needs, to our own 'tribe', or when we fail to grieve over injustice, racism and violence among nations and against persons. Such prayers settle for petty goals and produce religious infants.

One classic contest in the Bible between God and a god occurs in Exodus. Through the burning bush that was not consumed, God arrested Moses' attention. He told Moses to go back to Egypt and lead the children of Israel out of slavery.

Moses was no fool. He knew the children of Israel were not ready for self-government. More importantly, he understood Egyptian power. From the time he was a child, Moses had been acquainted with Egyptian grandeur and the Egyptian army.

Moses possessed a staff, a family and some sheep. When God told him to go tell Pharaoh to 'let my people go', Moses basically asked God, 'And when I arrive in Egypt, who do I tell the people and Pharaoh is my backer? Who should I say has sent me?'

That was a very important question. In Egypt, Pharaoh was considered a personification of the Egyptian god, which is how the people thought of him.

God answered Moses, 'Tell Pharaoh that "I AM WHO I AM" has sent you' (Exod. 3:13–15, author's paraphrase). From the Hebrew letters in 'I AM WHO I AM' we derive the word Yahweh, the name for God. Some incorrect grammar can make the point. God said, 'I is.' No matter how big and powerful the Pharaoh might be, the 'I AM' God had placed boundaries around him. God trumps Pharaoh every time. Through Moses, the 'I AM' God would convince Pharaoh he was no god at all. God would show Pharaoh just how dependent he really was. Even the mighty Pharaoh depended upon the 'I AM' for his existence.

The famous plagues (Exod. 7:8–11:10) were not meant to dazzle Pharaoh. The plagues showed that the Creator God places boundaries on even His highest rivals. God exposes even mighty Egypt's deity as powerless before the Eternal One who 'IS'. Ten times God overcame the Pharaoh. Each plague placed a boundary around something the Pharaoh thought he controlled. Finally, God killed the Pharaoh's firstborn son, who upon Pharaoh's death was supposed to become 'God's' embodiment. But now he was dead.

What is true of the Pharaoh is true of all gods, including the ones that invite us to pray to, serve and worship them. Even the Baal gods that supposedly controlled the weather and fertility in nature and humans, had to admit their bankruptcy. Elijah saw to that. When the Baal priests prayed for fire to fall on their sacrifice, nothing happened. But when Elijah prayed, God sent fire that consumed the sacrifice, the altar and the water Elijah had poured on the sacrifice (1 Kings 18). Shortly afterwards, God sent rains upon the parched land.

THE GOD WHO TAKES US DEEPER

Christian prayer is grounded in and directed towards the God who is beyond all gods. Mature Christian prayer has no place for a substitute Jesus. In an expression of true worship, mature Christian prayer is content to let God be God on His own terms. Faith in and prayer directed towards the God who 'IS' will never fail, because they're anchored in the One who provides His own being, His own life. The Bible never stops distinguishing between the living God and the gods. The gods are just images of human nature or subhuman powers that people elevate to a realm they can never successfully occupy. They are finite and will always disappear. Proclaiming that infinite distinction was one major role of the prophets.

Unlike the gods, God doesn't have to draw upon existing things for His security. He is life. He is spirit. He is power. He is grace. He is love. He is eternal. His faithfulness to Himself and to us is everlasting. He is Lord and Father. He is the One beside whom there is no other. He is the One who became incarnate in Jesus of Nazareth. This God 'became flesh and made his dwelling among us. We have seen his glory, the glory of the One and Only, who came from the Father, full of grace and truth ... From the fulness of his grace we have all received one blessing after another ... No-one has ever seen God, but God the One and Only, who is at the Father's side, has made him known' (John 1:14, 16, 18). 'God', said Karl Barth, 'is the One whose name and cause are borne by Jesus Christ.'[2]

This Christ in whom the very glory of the 'I AM WHO I AM' was manifest, is the One who taught us to pray, 'Our Father in heaven, hallowed be your name, your kingdom come, your will be done on earth as it is in heaven' (Matt. 6:9–10). I have heard many prayers and many requests for prayer in churches in which concerns for physical and material well-being far outweighed interest in the coming of the kingdom. Such prayers seemed to assign little interest to winning the lost or in being merciful and loving justice.

The writer to the Hebrews said that a Sabbath rest remains for the people of God (4:8–11). Part of what the Sabbath rest involves is arriving at a level of maturity in which the God with whom we commune, and the God we worship, is the God beyond all gods. This involves a depth of trust in God that doesn't scatter when things tremble. The rest He offers to His people passes all human understanding. It is a rest the gods cannot offer. This is the level at which faith and prayer are supposed to abide. There really is no other genuine rest, no other genuine peace. All the children of God have been invited to rest in the God beyond the gods. To this He calls us; He will empower us.

The God who is beyond all gods does not isolate Himself from us. He is the One who comes to us. Indeed, the God of Holy Scriptures is superior to humanity and the world. But He has also bound Himself to us. He is the faithful One. As the Lord and Shepherd of His people, He is also the world ruler, the Creator of all things, who shows His people what the 'gods' really are. He sets them free from the gods so that they may know Him, the only true and living One. To know Him is to have joy, peace and life everlasting.

Erik Routley wrote a hymn that expresses the Christian's trust in God:

New songs of celebration render
  To him who has great wonders done;
Awed by his love his foes surrender
  And fall before the Mighty One.
He has made his great salvation
  Which all his friends with joy confess;
He has revealed to every nation
  His everlasting righteousness.
Joyfully, heartily sounding
  Let every instrument and voice
Peal out the praise of grace abounding
  Calling the whole to rejoice.
Trumpets and organs set in motion
  Such sounds as make the heavens ring:
All things that live in earth and ocean

Make music for your mighty King.
Rivers and seas and torrents roaring,
    Honor the Lord with wild acclaim;
Mountains and stones look up adoring
    And find a voice to praise his name.
Righteous, commanding, ever glorious,
    Praises be that never cease;
Just is our God, whose truth victorious
    Established the world in peace.[3]

CONCLUSION

Tommy Dorsey (1899–1993) was widely acclaimed as 'the father of the gospel song'. Dorsey combined elements of the blues with traditional African-American religious music.

In 1932 Dorsey lost his wife and daughter in childbirth. His faith was tested. During his dark night of the soul, Dorsey wrote what became his most famous and influential song. In simple, plaintive language and with a tune that haunts the mind, Dorsey wrote, 'Take My Hand, Precious Lord'. The song is actually a prayer arising from a broken heart that has no exultant words of triumph to shout. All Dorsey had to offer the Lord is a simple expression of trust and hope.

In this book we have walked with those who cannot pray as others seem to be able to do. We have examined how the Lord walks with, or carries, them. No words seem more appropriate for concluding our journey together than the ones Tommy Dorsey penned years ago.

Precious Lord, take my hand,
Lead me on, let me stand.
I am tired, I am weak, I am worn.

Thro' the storm, thro' the night,
Lead me on to the light.
Take my hand, precious Lord; lead me home ...
When the darkness appears
And the night draws near,
And the day is past and gone,
At the river I stand;
Guide my feet, hold my hand.
Take my hand, precious Lord; lead me home.[4]

Notes

Chapter 1

1. Bernhard Anderson, *Understanding the Old Testament* (Englewood Cliffs, N.J.: Prentice-Hall, 1975), p.361.

2. Paul Ricoeur, *The Symbolism of Evil* (Boston: Beacon Press, 1969).

3. Philip Yancey, *Disappointment with God* (New York: Harper Paperbacks, 1988), p.24.

4. Marjorie Hewitt Suchocki, *In God's Presence: Theological Reflections on Prayer* (St. Louis: Chalice Press, 1996), p.2.

5. Mark Twain, 'The War Prayer', located at <www.lnstar.com/mall/literature/warpray.htm>.

Chapter 2

1. Matt. 6:5–6; 7:7–11; 18:19–20; Mark 11:22–25; John 14:13–14; 15:7; Acts 9:40; 12:5–11; Rom. 1:10; 2 Cor. 1:11; Phil. 4:6–7; Col. 1:9–12; James 5:13–18; 1 John 5:14–15.

2. *Luther's Works*, vol. 7, ed. Jaraslov Pelikin (St. Louis: Concordia Press, 1970), p.159.

3. John H. Wright, S.J., *A Theology of Christian Prayer* (New York: Pueblo Publishing Co., 1979), pp.71–72.

4. Donald G. Bloesch, *The Struggle of Prayer* (San Francisco: Harper and Row, 1980), p.71.

5. Wright, *A Theology of Christian Prayer*, pp.74–75.

6. Ibid., p.75.

7. Bloesch, *The Struggle of Prayer*, pp.86–90.

8. Karl Barth, *Prayer*, trans. Sarah F. Terrien (Philadelphia: Westminster Press, 1952), p.21. Quoted in Bloesch, p.74.

9. Bloesch, *The Struggle of Prayer*, p.72.

10. P. T. Forsyth, *The Soul of Prayer*, 5th ed. (London: Independent Press, 1966), p.79. Quoted in Bloesch, p.75.

11. Harry Emerson Fosdick, *The Meaning of Prayer* (New York: Association Press, 1916), p.63. Quoted in Bloesch, p.74.

12. William Law, *The Spirit of Prayer and the Spirit of Love*, ed. Sidney Spencer (Canterbury: Clarke, 1969), p.120. Quoted in Bloesch, p.74.

13. Bloesch, *The Struggle of Prayer*, p.74.

14. Ibid., p.87.

15. Ibid.

16. Elsie Gibson, *Honest Prayer* (Philadelphia: Westminster Press, 1981), p.60.

17. Suchocki, *In God's Presence*, p.18.

Chapter 3

1. C.S. Lewis, *The Screwtape Letters* (New York: New American Library, 1988), p.16.

Chapter 4

1. Annie Dillard, *Pilgrim at Tinker Creek* (New York: Harper's Magazine Press, 1974), pp.5–6.

2. Anderson, *Understanding the Old Testament,* p.512.

Chapter 5

1. Herman Melville, 'Bartleby the Scrivener', *Literature of Western Civilization,* vol. 2, ed. Louis G. Locke, John Pendy Kirby, and M.E. Porter (New York: Ronald Press Company, 1952), pp.415–31.

2. Frederick Buechner, *Telling the Truth: The Gospel as Tragedy, Comedy, and Fairy Tale* (New York: Harper and Row, 1977), pp.33–35.

3. From *Doubters and Dreamers,* by Bill Comeau. Copyright © 1973 by The Upper Room. Used by permission of Upper Room Books.

4. Anderson, *Understanding the Old Testament,* p.453.

Chapter 6

1. 'Macedonian Village Is Center of Europe Web in Sex Trade', *New York Times* on the Web, International Section, 28 July, 2001.

2. Dillard, *Pilgrim at Tinker Creek*, p.170.

3. Ibid., p.168.

4. Ibid., p.131.

5. Ibid., p.132.

6. Ibid., p.134.

7. Ibid., p.28.

8. Ibid., p.33.

9. Ibid., p.271.

10. Ibid., p.265.

11. Ibid., p.176.

12. Ibid., p.161.

13. Ibid., p.176.

14. Ibid., p.264.

15. Ibid.

16. *New York Times* on the Web, 7 July, 2001.

17. Dillard, *Pilgrim at Tinker Creek*, p.31.

18. Ibid., p.33.

19. Hendrik Berkhof, *Christ and the Powers*, trans. John H. Yoder (Scottdale, Pa.: Herald Press, 1977), p.38.

20. Dillard, *Pilgrim at Tinker Creek*, p.268.

21. Berkhof, *Christ and the Powers*, p.40.

22. Ibid., p.43.

23. Ibid., p.44.

24. Karl Barth, *Church Dogmatics: A Selection*, with an introduction by Helmut Gollwitzer (Louisville, Ky.: Westminster John Knox Press, 1994), pp.116–17. Selection from *CD* III, 2, p.148 f.

Chapter 7

1. From the *Boston Globe*, 16 March, 2001, B1, B4.

2. 'The Road Ahead', from *Thoughts in Solitude*, by Thomas Merton. Copyright © 1958 by the Abbey of Our Lady of Gethsemani. Copyright renewed 1986 by the Trustees of the Thomas Merton Legacy Trust. Reprinted by permission of Farrar, Straus and Giroux, LLC.

Chapter 8

1. *Classics Devotional Bible* (Grand Rapids: Zondervan Publishing House, 1996), p.208.

2. Ibid., p.882.

3. Barth, *Church Dogmatics: Selections*, 71. Selection from *CD* IV, 2, p.303 f.

4. Sources consulted: *The Expositor's Bible Commentary* (Zondervan); *The Anchor Bible* (Doubleday); *The Century Bible* (Thomas Nelson); *New Century Bible* (Butler and Tanner); *Word Bible Commentary* (Word); *Baker Exegetical Commentary on the New Testament* (Baker Books); *The New International Commentary on the New Testament: The Gospel According to John*, rev. ed. (Leon Morris, William B. Eerdmans); and *The Gospel According to John*, D.A. Carson (InterVarsity Press).

Chapter 9

1. This story is based on an article by Karen Davies, 'Arab Masters Do as They Please', and other news accounts of the slave trade in southern Sudan. Davis's article was written for the Associated Press. It is located on the Project Open Book web site at <www.domini.org/openbook/home.htm>

2.   *Black Voices,* ed. Abraham Chapman (New York: Mentor Books, 1968), p.362.

Chapter 10

1.   Leo Tolstoy, *The Death of Ivan Illich* trans. Louise and Aylmer Maude, dist. by Tolstoi Library <http://home.aol.com/tolstoy28>
E-mail: tolstoy28@aol.com.
2.   *The Book of Prayers: Compiled for Everyday Worship,* ed. Leon and Elfreda McCauley (New York: Avenel Books, 1954), pp.79–80.
3.   Ibid., p.79.
4.   Ibid., p.80.
5.   Taken from *The Compassionate Friends* (Independence, MO 64052), July–August 2001.
6.   *The Book of Prayers,* p.80.

Chapter 11

1.   *Collected Works of Flannery O'Connor,* ed. Sally Fitzgerald (New York: Library of America, dist. by Viking Press, 1988), p.1067.
2.   Karl Barth, *Church Dogmatics: Selections*, 30. Selection from *CD* III, 4, p.479 f.
3.   Words: Erik Routley. © 1974 Hope Publishing Co., Carol Stream, IL 60188. All rights reserved. Used by permission.
4.   'Precious Lord, Take My Hand', words and music by THOMAS A. DORSEY. © 1938 (renewed) WARNER-TAMER-LANE PUBLISHING CORP. in the U.S.A. and UNICHAPPELL MUSIC INC. elsewhere throughout the world. All rights reserved. Lyrics reprinted with permission from Warner Bros. Publications, Miami, FL 33014.

National Distributors

UK: (and countries not listed below)
CWR, Waverley Abbey House, Waverley Lane, Farnham, Surrey GU9 8EP.
Tel: (01252) 784700 Outside UK +44 1252 784700
AUSTRALIA: CMC Australasia, PO Box 519, Belmont, Victoria 3216.
Tel: (03) 5241 3288
CANADA: Cook Communications Ministries, PO Box 98, 55 Woodslee Avenue,
Paris, Ontario. Tel: 1800 263 2664
GHANA: Challenge Enterprises of Ghana, PO Box 5723, Accra.
Tel: (021) 222437/223249 Fax: (021) 226227
HONG KONG: Cross Communications Ltd, 1/F, 562A Nathan Road, Kowloon.
Tel: 2780 1188 Fax: 2770 6229
INDIA: Crystal Communications, 10-3-18/4/1, East Marredpalli,
Secunderabad – 500026, Andhra Pradesh. Tel/Fax: (040) 27737145
KENYA: Keswick Books and Gifts Ltd, PO Box 10242, Nairobi.
Tel: (02) 331692/226047 Fax: (02) 728557
MALAYSIA: Salvation Book Centre (M) Sdn Bhd, 23 Jalan SS 2/64,
47300 Petaling Jaya, Selangor.
Tel: (03) 78766411/78766797 Fax: (03) 78757066/78756360
NEW ZEALAND: CMC Australasia, PO Box 36015, Lower Hutt.
Tel: 0800 449 408 Fax: 0800 449 049
NIGERIA: FBFM, Helen Baugh House, 96 St Finbarr's College Road, Akoka,
Lagos. Tel: (01) 7747429/4700218/825775/827264
PHILIPPINES: OMF Literature Inc, 776 Boni Avenue, Mandaluyong City.
Tel: (02) 531 2183 Fax: (02) 531 1960
SINGAPORE: Armour Publishing Pte Ltd, Block 203A Henderson Road,
11–06 Henderson Industrial Park, Singapore 159546.
Tel: 6 276 9976 Fax: 6 276 7564
SOUTH AFRICA: Struik Christian Books, 80 MacKenzie Street, PO Box 1144,
Cape Town 8000. Tel: (021) 462 4360 Fax: (021) 461 3612
SRI LANKA: Christombu Books, 27 Hospital Street, Colombo 1.
Tel: (01) 433142/328909
TANZANIA: CLC Christian Book Centre, PO Box 1384, Mkwepu Street, Dar es
Salaam. Tel/Fax: (022) 2119439
USA: Cook Communications Ministries, PO Box 98, 55 Woodslee Avenue, Paris,
Ontario, Canada. Tel: 1800 263 2664
ZIMBABWE: Word of Life Books, Shop 4, Memorial Building,
35 S Machel Avenue, Harare. Tel: (04) 781305 Fax: (04) 774739
For email addresses, visit the CWR website: www.cwr.org.uk
CWR is a registered charity – number 294387

Day and Residential Courses
Counselling Training
Leadership Development
Biblical Study Courses
Regional Seminars
Ministry to Women
Daily Devotionals
Books and Videos
Conference Centre

Trusted all Over the World

CWR HAS GAINED A WORLDWIDE
reputation as a centre of excellence for
Bible-based training and resources. From
our headquarters at Waverley Abbey
House, Farnham, England, we have
been serving God's people for 40 years
with a vision to help apply God's Word
to everyday life and relationships. The
daily devotional *Every Day with Jesus* is
read by over three-quarters of a million
people in more than 150 countries, and
our unique courses in biblical studies and
pastoral care are respected all over the
world. Waverley Abbey House provides a
conference centre in a tranquil setting.

For free brochures on our seminars and
courses, conference facilities, or a catalogue
of CWR resources, please contact us at the
following address.
**CWR, Waverley Abbey House, Waverley
Lane, Farnham, Surrey GU9 8EP, UK**

Telephone: +44 (0)1252 784700
Email: mail@cwr.org.uk
Website: www.cwr.org.uk